The Life and Times of Benjamin Franklin

Professor H.W. Brands
Texas A&M University

The Life and Times of Benjamin Franklin
Professor H.W. Brands

Executive Producer
John J. Alexander

Executive Editor
Donna F. Carnahan

RECORDING
Producer - David Markowitz
Director - Matt Cavnar

COURSE GUIDE
Editor - Edward White
Contributing Editors - James Gallagher
Karen Sparrough
Michael Tennyson

Lecture content ©2003 by H.W. Brands
Course Guide ©2003 by Recorded Books, LLC
℗2003 by Recorded Books, LLC
#UT029 ISBN: 1-4025-5883-X

Course Syllabus

The Life and Times of Benjamin Franklin

About Your Professor — H.W. Brands

Professor H.W. Brands of Austin, Texas, a prolific and award-winning writer, is currently Distinguished Professor of History and holder of the Melbern G. Glasscock Chair in American History at Texas A&M in College Station, Texas.

Brands was born in Portland, Oregon. He attended Stanford University, receiving a B.A. in history in 1975. He was a traveling salesman for a year before taking up teaching at Jesuit High School in Portland, where he taught history and mathematics for five years.

Meanwhile Brands earned graduate degrees from Reed College (M.A. in liberal studies, 1978) and Portland State University (M.S. in mathematics, 1981). In 1981 he relocated to Austin, Texas, where he received a Ph.D. in history from the University of Texas in 1985.

He worked as an oral historian at the University of Texas Law School for a year, then became a visiting assistant professor of history at Vanderbilt University in Nashville, Tennessee. In 1987 he joined the history faculty at Texas A&M University in College Station, where he has been ever since, with the exception of a semester as a visiting professor at the University of Texas at Austin.

In addition to teaching, Brands coordinates the History of the Americas Research Program at Texas A&M University and is the editor of the *Series in Foreign Relations* at Texas A&M Press and associate editor of *Presidential Studies Quarterly.*

Brands is the author of seventeen books, has edited four others, and has published dozens of articles and scores of reviews.

His most recent works include *Woodrow Wilson 1913-1921: The American Presidents Series* (Times Books), now available in bookstores, and *The Age of Gold* (Doubleday), also available in bookstores (paperback version due in bookstores October 2003).

Other books include *The Strange Death of American Liberalism, The First American, TR: The Last Romantic, What America Owes the World, The Reckless Decade,* and *The Devil We Knew.*

Brands is a contributor to the *New York Times,* the *Wall Street Journal,* the *Washington Post,* the *International Herald Tribune,* the *Boston Globe,* the *National Interest,* the *American Historical Review,* the *Journal of American History,* the *Political Science Quarterly,* and *American History.*

He has also written for the *Oxford Companion to the Second World War, Oxford Companion to Military History, Encyclopedia of U.S. Foreign Relations,* and the *American Heritage Encyclopedia of American History.*

Brands is frequently interviewed by the American and foreign press, including PBS, ABC, MSNBC, A&E/History Channel, BBC, NPR, Australian Broadcasting Company, the *Wall Street Journal, USA Today,* and the *Philadelphia Inquirer.*

The First American was a finalist for the Pulitzer Prize and the *Los Angeles Times* Prize, as well as a *New York Times* bestseller. *What America Owes the World* was a finalist for the Lionel Gelber Prize.

"Benjamin Franklin Drawing Electricity from the Sky"
by Benjamin West, ca. 1816

Introduction

Chandler, balladeer, poet, printer, writer, humorist, satirist, swimmer, businessman, inventor, philosopher, soldier, administrator, scientist, politician, lady's man, musician, humanitarian, philanthropist—it's almost easier to list the things Franklin was *not* than try to explain the pursuits and interests of his many-faceted life.

In this course we will study in some detail the life of Benjamin Franklin and his influence on both American and world history. From his early days as a printer's apprentice to very nearly his last days, Benjamin Franklin's thirst for knowledge and his desire to share what he knew brought him into the forefront of a changing world. His contributions through inventions, scientific investigation, and political thought still echo over two-hundred years after his passing.

A man of his time and of his place, Benjamin Franklin sought not only to enlighten himself, but also to help shed a new light of reason and self-government to all who would pay heed.

Lecture 1: Out of Boston: 1706-1723
Birth to Age 17

Before beginning this lecture you may want to . . .

Read H.W. Brands' The First American, Chapter 1.

Introduction:

The 18th century was a period of great worldwide innovation, discovery, and change. One of the great reflections of this change could be seen in America, where a group of thirteen colonies that began the century as parts of the empire of Great Britain came to see themselves as a united, independent, and separate nation. At the heart of this political change—and clearly reflecting the scientific and social change of his century—was Benjamin Franklin. To study Franklin's life is to learn not only the history of a single man, but to understand some of the most monumental changes in all of history.

Consider this . . .
1. What aspects of Franklin's life reflected events and perceptions throughout the American colonies and the world of the 18th century?
2. How did the background of Franklin's family serve as a reflection of the type of person he would become?

I. **Franklin is an important person to study today because of the way he reflected America during the century of the nation's founding.**

   A. His life coincides with the 18th century, a critical period in American history, revealing the times from both a public and personal angle.

      1. He was born in the first decade of the century and died in the century's final decade.

      2. Born in an age of superstition, he died in the age of reason.

   B. His life's journey (from Boston to Philadelphia to London to Paris and back to Philadelphia) tracks the high points of American history during this period, helping us to understand how America became the nation that it was to become.

   C. Various aspects of Franklin's character set standards for what would later be perceived as the American character.

      1. Practicality

      2. Ambition

      3. Optimism

      4. Self-improvement

   D. He was the most engaging of the Founding Fathers.

      1. He comes across as the only one most contemporary people feel they could clap on the shoulder, buy a beer for, and shoot the breeze with.

      2. Other Founding Fathers appear to be made of marble; Franklin is flesh and blood.

E. Nearly everyone has some conventional notions of Franklin.

II. **Boston at the beginning of the 18th century was still a community dominated by the Puritan ethics and superstitions of its founders.**

  A. The Salem witch trials from the previous century still haunted the community.

    1. These actions had been discredited by the time of Franklin's birth.

    2. But many who had taken part were still alive and still fearful of witches.

  B. Cotton Mather and other Puritan elders governed with a firm, holy hand.

  C. A town by the sea, with the world coming and going, it was the busiest seaport in North America.

    1. It was the hub of commerce for the region.

    2. People like Franklin grew up with an awareness that they were part of a wider world.

  D. A very literate community, it was the best place in the colonies for printers.

    1. Multiple copies of Sunday sermons needed reproduction.

    2. Preachers like Mather published their sermons regularly.

III. **Franklin's family had left England for religious reasons.**

  A. Josiah, a candlemaker, married Abiah, his second wife, after the death of his first wife.

    1. Franklin was descended from dissenters on both sides

    2. This background shaped Franklin's own later penchant for dissent.

  B. Franklin was born January 1706.

    1. He was the eighth child of his mother.

    2 He was the fifteenth child (tenth son) of his father.

    3. Being one of the youngest of a very large family, Franklin realized he had

Benjamin Franklin Selling His Own Ballads

BEN FRANKLIN – POET

As a young man, Ben Franklin was a voracious reader, which, in turn, led to his writing. He began with poetry at an early age. The following is a verse written to commemorate the killing of Edward Teach, commonly called Blackbeard.

Will you hear of a bloody battle
Lately fought upon the seas,
It will make your ears to rattle,
And your admiration cease.
Have you heard of Teach the Rover
And his knavery on the main,
How of gold he was a lover,
How he loved all ill-got gain.

And after several more stanzas:

Teach and Maynard on the quarter,
Fought it out most manfully;
Maynard's sword did cut him shorter,
Losing his head he there did die.

Of his poetry Franklin said . . .

"They were wretched stuff, in the Grub-street-ballad style; and when they were printed he sent me about the town to sell them.
The first sold wonderfully, the event being recent, having made a great noise. This flattered my vanity; but my father discouraged me by ridiculing my performances, and telling me verse-makers were generally beggars. So I escaped being a poet, most probably a very bad one."

to get along with people to make his way in the world.

C. Franklin claimed he could not remember a time when he couldn't read.

   1. His talent for learning made his father think he would make a good minister.

   2. Franklin was pulled out of formal schooling after two years when Josiah decided the investment wasn't worth the expense.

   3. His lack of formal education made Franklin more open to learning everything and to teaching himself new things throughout his life.

IV. **Franklin came to his life's vocation as a printer almost by accident.**

A. He threatened to run away to sea if he was forced to continue working in his father's candleshop.

APPRENTICESHIP

As a youth, Ben Franklin dreamed of going to sea as a cabin boy, an ambition vehemently opposed by his father, who attempted to find his son an apprenticeship with various craftsmen in Boston, such as a local cutler and later a chandler. Eventually, at the age of twelve, Ben went to work for his brother, James, a printer.

His term of service was initially for nine years, longer than most apprenticeships of the time, but typical of the greater needs of the printing trade. In addition, James promised to pay him at the journeyman's level during the final year of his service.

Ben found the job's requirements of manual dexterity, physical strength, proofreading, and intelligence to be an excellent fit for his growing energies and abilities. These abilities also benefited from the access Ben had to various important books of the time, such as John Bunyan's *Pilgrim's Progress,* Plutarch's *Lives,* Daniel Defoe's *Essay on Projects,* and the sermons of Cotton Mather.

Ben became friends with local booksellers and customers of his brother, who allowed him to read from their stock, after hours. He proved such an avid reader that at times he would skip meals in order to use the money saved to buy books.

James didn't mind his younger brother's efforts at personal development, as he was able to balance these activities with the requirements of the job. He even printed some of Ben's early efforts at poetry, an experiment that eventually was relinquished in favor of prose.

Franklin As An Apprentice

© Bettmann/CORBIS

Among his contributions were a series of some letters written secretly, under the persona of a woman named Silence Dogood. They dealt with topical matters of the day and proved so popular that James, who was unaware that his younger brother was the author, was heard at one point to urge "Mistress Dogood" to write more.

Eventually Ben was discovered to be the author, and the resulting uproar caused a break with both his father (who took James's side) and his brother, who soon had Ben blacklisted from working for any other printer in Boston. Finally, in 1723, Ben left his apprenticeship early and moved to Philadelphia, where his future began.

1. His eldest brother had been lost at sea.
2. Josiah feared this might happen to Ben.
B. Eventually apprenticed to his brother James, a printer, Ben found an occupation that perfectly matched his skills and temperament.
1. Printing required a mastery of reading and writing.
2. It required manual dexterity in setting type.
3. It required physical strength and stamina.
4. It needed an artistic eye.
5. It required a business sense.
C. Ben had a strained, if effective, working relationship with his brother.
1. James demanded respect as both master and elder brother.
2. Ben was not always compliant.
3. Ben's earliest published writing appeared in James's paper.
4. Ben's teenage poetry was popular enough that it was used to sell newspapers.
5. Ben realized he was more talented than James and wanted a larger role in producing the paper.

V. **Ben's desire for an increased role in printing the newspaper led to trouble in the shop.**
A. Ben created the persona of Silence Dogood to discuss life in New England.
1. Readers loved Silence Dogood's letters.
2. Circulation boomed.
3. James, unaware that his own brother had written under this pseudonym, publicly called for more letters.
B. After six months, James discovered Ben's ruse; fisticuffs followed.
C. Ben appealed to his father, who backed James.

VI. **His dispute with James caused Ben to flee Boston.**
A. Convinced that he was smarter than James, but would always be under his thumb, Ben tried to break his indenture.
B. James, anticipating this, persuaded fellow printers to blacklist Ben.
C. Ben also chafed at Puritan orthodoxy, sensing trouble if he stayed in Boston.
D. Ben and his friend cooked up a story of having gotten a girl pregnant, finding a ship's captain sympathetic to this type of situation.
E. In September 1723, at seventeen, Franklin fled Boston to seek his fortune in the wide world.

Summary: Benjamin Franklin was born at a time and in a place where great change was imminent. As a reflection of that time and place—and through his own genius and work ethic—he grew to embody what by the end of the 18th century would be considered the American spirit.

The Letters of Silence Dogood . . .

For one year the sixteen-year-old Franklin wrote for his brother's paper as "Silence Dogood." He delivered fifteen letters in all filled with witty diatribes and many ideas that would have gotten him in trouble with the authorities. The following is from an issue of *The New-England Courant* (from Monday, May 21 to Monday, May 28,1722).

To the Author of the New-England Courant.

SIR,

I SHALL here Present your Readers with a Letter from one, who informs me that I have begun at the wrong End of my business, and that I ought to begin at Home, and censure the Vices and Follies of my own Sex, before I venture to meddle with your's: Neverthless, I am resolved to declare this Speculation to the Fair Tribe, and endeavour to show, that Mr. Ephraim charges Women with being particularly guilty of Pride, Idleness, &c. wrongfully, inasmuch as the Men have not only as great a Share in those Vice as the Women, but are likewise in a great a Share in those Vice as the Women, but are likewise in a great Measure the Cause of that which the Women are guilty of. I think it will be best to produce my Antagonist, before I encounter him.

To Mrs. DOGOOD

Madam, My Design in troubling you with this Letter is, to de'sire you would begin with your own Sex first: Let the first Volley of your Resentments be directed against Female Vice; let Female Idleness, Ignorance and Folly, (which are Vices more peculiar to your Sex than to our's,) be the Subject of your Satyrs, but more especially Female Pride, which I think is intollerable. Here is a large Field 'that wants Cultivation,' and which I believe you are able (if willing) to improve with Advantage; and when you have once reformed the Women, you will find it a much easier Tasker to reform the Men, because Women are the prime Causes of a great many Male Enormities. This is all at present from

Your Friendly Wellwisher.

Ephraim Cesorious.

And the Response from Silence . . .

After Thanks to My Correspondent for his kindness in cutting out Work for me, I must assure him, that I find it a very different Matter to reprove Women separate from The Men: for what Vice is there in which the Men have they not a far greater, as in Drunkenness, Swearing, &c. And if they have, then it follows, that when a Vice is to be reproved, Men who are most culpable, deserve the most Reprehension, and certainly therefore, ought to have it. But we will waive this Point at present, and proceed to a particular Consideration of what my Correspondent calls Female Vice.

As for Idleness, if should Quaere, Where are the greatest Number of its Votaries to be found, with us or the Men? it might I believe be easily and truly answer'd, With the latter. For notwithstanding the Men are commonly complaining how hard they are forc'd to labour, only to Maintain their Wifes in Pomp and Idleness, yet if you go among the Women, you will learn, that they have always more Work upon their Hands than they are able to do; and that a Woman's Work is never done, &c. But however, Suppose we should grant for once, that we are generally more idle than the Men, (without making any Allowance for the Weakness of the Sex) I desire to know whose Fault it is. Are not the Men to blame for their Folly in maintaining us in Idleness? Who is there that can be handsomely supported in Assurance, Ease and Pleasure by another, that will chuse rather to earn his Bread by the Sweat of his own Brows? And if a Man will be so for food and so For Fish, as to labour hard himself for a Livelihood, and Suffer his Wise in the mean Time to fit in Ease and Idleness, let him not blame her if she does so, for it is in a great Measure his own Fault.

And now for the Ignorance and Folly which he reproaches us with, let us see if we are Fools and Ignoramus's Writer, having this subject in Hand, has the following Words, wherein he lays the Fault wholly on the Men, for not allowing Women the Advantages of Education.

I have (says he) often Thought of it as one of the most barbarous Customs in the World, considering us as a civiliz'd and Christian Country, that we deny the Advantages of Learning to Women. We reproach the Sex every Day with Folly and Impertinence, while I am confident, had they the Advantages of Education equal to us, they would be guilty of less than our selves. One would wonder indeed how it should happen that Women are conversible at all, since they are only beholding to natural Parts for all their Knowledge. Their Youth is spent to teach them to stitch and sow, or make Baubles: They are taught to read indeed, and perhaps to write their Names, or so and that is the Height of a Woman's Education. And I would but ask any who slight the Sex for their Understanding, What is a Man (a Gentleman, I mean) good for that is taught no more? If knowledge and Understanding had been useless Additions to the Sex God Almighty would never have given them Capacities, for he made nothing Needless. What has the Woman done to forfeit the Priviledge of being taught? Does she plague us with her Pride and Impertinence? Why did we not let her learn, that she might have had more Wit? Shall we upbraid Women with Folly, when 'tis only the Error of this inhumane Custom that hindred them being made wiser.

So much for Female Ignorance and Folly, and now let us a little consider the Pride which my Correspondent thinks is intollerable. By this Expression of his, one would think he is some dejected Swain, Tyranniz'd over by some cruel haughty Nymph, who (perhaps he thinks) has no more Reason to be proud than himself.

Alas-a-day! What shall we say in this Cafe! Why truly, if Women are proud, it is certainly owing to the Men still; for if they will be such Simpletons as to humble themselves at their Feet, and fill their credulous Ears with extravagant Praises of their Wilt, Beauty, and other Accomplishments (perhaps where there are none too) and when Women by this Means perswaded that they are Something more than humane, What Wonder is it, if they carry themselves haughtily, and live extravagantly. Notwithstanding, I believe there are more Instances of extravagent Pride to be found among Men than among Women, and this Fault is certainly more heinous in the former than in the latter.

Upon the whole, I conclude, that it will be impossible to last any Vice, of which the Men are not equally guilty with the Women, and consequently deserve an equal if not a greater) Share in the Censure. However I exhort both to amend, where both are culpable, otherwise they may expect to be severly handled by Sir,

Your Humble Servant.

SILENCE DOGOOD

THE NEW-ENGLAND COURANT

With the help of his friends, James Franklin began this paper on August 7, 1721. The paper's launch coincided with a smallpox epidemic that was ravaging Boston and dividing it as well over the issue of inoculation.

Established medical tradition and most Bostonians felt inoculation was an evil plot that actually spread smallpox. Boston's clergy, including the forceful Congregational minister, Cotton Mather, supported inoculation.

Dr. William Douglass, a friend of James Franklin's who opposed the practice, suggested that the paper be used to decrease the influence of preachers like Cotton Mather.

Inevitably, James found himself in the midst of the inoculation controversy. Much space in many of the early issues was devoted to the smallpox debate. And while the public sided with Franklin on the smallpox issue, many felt uneasy about Franklin's critical stance on the clergy.

During this time, James pressed on. He attempted to create his newspaper in the image of publications he had read or worked on while in London.

He published commentaries from people using such names as Timothy Turnstone, Ichabod Henroost, Betty Frugal, Tabitha Talkative, and Dorothy Love. They were eventually joined by the mysterious Silence Dogood, who also contributed columns on the topics of the day.

In the June 11, 1722 issue of the *Courant* ran this seemingly innocuous piece: "We are advised from Boston that the government of Massachusetts are fitting out a ship, to go after the pirates, to be commanded by Captain Peter Papillon, and 'tis thought he will sail some time this month, wind and weather permitting."

The governmental Council was insulted by the overtones that suggested cowardice and laziness, and gave James a two-week time-out in jail to think about his tart tongue. While James was imprisoned his sixteen-year-old brother Benjamin ran the paper.

But this was just the start of James's woes. In the January 14, 1723 issue an "Essay Against Hypocrites" was published. Though not named directly, most readers recognized the target of the *Courant's* jolting to be Cotton Mather. So did the committee of the House who barred James Franklin from publishing.

Cotton Mather
(1663-1728)

The House charged that "the Tendency of the said Paper is to mock Religion, and bring it into Contempt, that the Holy Scriptures are therefore profanely abused, that the Reverend and faithful Ministers of the Gospel are injuriously Reflected on, His Majesty's Government affronted, and the Peace and good Order of His Majesty's Subjects of this Province disturbed, by the said *Courant*."

In the January 28 issue, Franklin published a faux retraction and made use of a flimsy scheme in the words of his younger brother Ben. The *Courant* was now advertised as being printed by Benjamin Franklin. By this time the younger brother was running out of patience with James.

Finally, on September 30, an ad in the *Courant* read, "James Franklin, printer, in Queen's Street, wants a likely lad for an apprentice." Benjamin had run away. Boston's loss would be the City of Brotherly Love's gain, all thanks to an unloving older brother.

James Franklin tried to keep the *Courant* going. But constant battles with more conservative and puritanical Boston wore him down. After the 255th issue of the *Courant*, dated June 25, 1726, James Franklin folded the paper. He moved to Rhode Island seeking a more liberal environment and died there in 1735.

FOR GREATER UNDERSTANDING

Consider

1. How much do you think Franklin's lack of formal education contributed to his lifelong love of learning?
2. Which aspects of Franklin's youthful personality were most responsible for his success?
3. Would Franklin have achieved the same kind of international acclaim in life had he stayed in Boston?

Suggested Reading

Brands, H.W. The First American: The Life and Times of Benjamin Franklin. New York: Doubleday, 2000.

Other Books of Interest

Franklin, Benjamin. Autobiography of Benjamin Franklin and Other Writings. New York: Penguin USA, 1989.

Franklin, Benjamin. Papers of Benjamin Franklin: January 6, 1706 through December 31, 1939, Vol. 1. Leonard W. Labaree (ed.) New Haven: Yale University Press, 1959.

Websites to Visit

1. http://www.historycarper.com/resources/twobf1/contents.htm - On-line copies of the letters of Silence Dogood.
2. http://www.ushistory.org/franklin/courant/ - Issues of The New-England Courant on-line.
3. http://www.ushistory.org/franklin/ - The Electric Franklin.

Recorded Books

Brands, H.W. The First American: The Life and Times of Benjamin Franklin. Narrated by Nelson Runger. UNABRIDGED. Recorded Books, 2000 (2 cassettes/36.75 hours).

Franklin, Benjamin. The Autobiography of Benjamin Franklin. Narrated by Adrian Cronauer. UNABRIDGED. Recorded Books, 1986 (4 cassettes/5.5 hours).

Franklin, Benjamin. Benjamin Franklin: Diplomat. Narrated by Adrian Cronauer. UNABRIDGED. Recorded Books (3 cassettes/4.75 hours).

Franklin, Benjamin. Benjamin Franklin: On Love, Marriage & Other Matters. Narrated by Adrian Cronauer. UNABRIDGED. Recorded Books (3 cassettes/3.5 hours).

Hawke, David Freeman. Franklin. Narrated by Nelson Runger. UNABRIDGED. Recorded Books (12 cassettes/16.25 hours).

To order Recorded Books, call 1-800-638-1304 or go to www.recordedbooks.com. Also available for rental.

Before beginning this lecture you may want to . . .

Read H.W. Brands' The First American, Chapters 2-3.

Introduction:

In Philadelphia, Franklin found a city nearly perfectly suited to his temperament and work ethic. Despite some brief false starts, particularly in the area of work, he soon settled into his new life in the city that would forever after remain most closely connected to his name.

Consider this . . .

1. How did Franklin react to early disappointments he faced in trying to establish himself as a printer after leaving Boston?

2. What aspects of Philadelphia were more suited to Franklin's personality than Boston?

I. **The journey south from Boston taught Franklin some life lessons.**

A. When his ship became becalmed, he learned a lesson in flexibility when he was forced to fall off the vegetarian wagon.

B. He learned the difference between religious colonies and commercial colonies when he found no work as a printer in New York, since the local burghers were too busy making money to read.

C. When a printer suggested that his son, in Philadelphia, might have work, Franklin showed his survival ability when he nearly drowned in the Hudson, got soaked while walking across New Jersey, and rowed down the Delaware.

II. **The city of the Friends matched Franklin's temperament nicely.**

A. He arrived inauspiciously in October 1723.

1. He had only a dollar in his pocket, not knowing a soul in the city or the province.

2. He was legally a fugitive.

B. Philadelphia—the brainchild of William Penn and a refuge for Quakers and other dissenters—was the perfect spot for a freethinker like Franklin.

C. From the very beginning, Franklin found Philadelphia different from Boston.

1. He found a haven for dissenters by following Quakers to their meeting, where they let him sleep through services.

2. He followed his nose to a bakery, where he discovered that the bread was different than in Boston.

3. He bought three puffy rolls, then wandered up Market Street, dirty and wet and cold from the journey, with dirty linen hanging from his pockets.

4. He passed the home of John Read, where fifteen-year-old Deborah Read noticed him. She would later become his wife.

D. Franklin sized up the two printers in town, unimpressed.

    1. Franklin chose to work with Samuel Keimer, an eccentric but pleasant man.

    2. He took a room with John Read, his future father-in-law.

III. **His lack of enthusiasm for his job in Philadelphia led Franklin on a brief London detour.**

A. William Keith, the governor of the province, was impressed with Franklin and encouraged him to establish his own print shop.

B. Franklin tried to get capital from Josiah in Boston, but his father was unimpressed.

C. Keith suggested that Franklin travel to London to purchase type and other supplies on Keith's credit.

    1. Franklin arrived in London at the age of eighteen.

    2. He discovered that Keith had no London credit.

Franklin Gardening

To save money for books and improve his health, Franklin became a vegetarian for a time while in London.

D. Stranded in the great capital of the greatest empire on earth, Franklin discovered a taste for the pleasures of the big city.

    1. He partook of theater, taverns, and houses of prostitution ("foolish intrigues with low women").

    2. He found work among London printers, which extended his education in his craft.

E. He tried to avoid paying into a beer fund, wanting to save the money.

    1. He disliked what the heavy drinking did to his fellows' work.

    2. They sabotaged his own work and he eventually gave in on this point.

F. He engaged in the intellectual life of London.

    1. He composed "A Dissertation on Liberty and Necessity, Pleasure and Pain."

2. He made a name for himself among dissenters.

G. His teaching of swimming to make some extra money made him a favorite of the gentry.

IV. **Despite the pleasures of London, Franklin was eager to return to America.**

A. After saving his money, he bought passage for America.

B. During a long and difficult voyage, he continued his education.

1. He examined sea life.

2. He studied his fellow passengers.

3. He observed eclipses of the sun and moon.

C. Finally reaching the estuary of the Delaware River, he received an offer of faster passage for the final leg. "We accepted of their kind proposal, and about ten o'clock landed at Philadelphia, heartily congratulating each other upon our having happily completed so tedious and dangerous a voyage. Thank God!"

Summary: In running from his situation in Boston, Franklin chanced upon the city of Philadelphia, which was perfectly suited to his personality and goals. Despite having to overcome some initial obstacles, Franklin would forever after be closely associated with the city he made his home.

Old English Custom House Portsmouth, England, ca. 1730

© Stapleton Collection/CORBIS

FOR GREATER UNDERSTANDING

Consider

1. What role does accident and chance—such as Franklin's inability to find work in New York—play in history?

2. What other historical figures do you closely associate with a particular city? What does this association tell you about both the figures and the cities?

Suggested Reading

Cohn, Ellen R., (et al.) Editors. The Papers of Benjamin Franklin—Volume I. New Haven, CT: Yale University Press & American Philosophical Society, 2002.

Franklin, Benjamin. A Dissertation On Liberty, Necessity, Pleasure, And Pain (Notable American Authors). Reprint Services Corp.

Other Books of Interest

Thevenot, Melchisedec. Art of Swimming Sixteen Ninety Six. Manchester, NH: Ayer Company Publishers; 3rd edition, 1972.

Websites to Visit

1. http://ballindalloch-press.com/society/index.html - Website of "The Society of 18th Century Gentlemen," a club devoted to replicating life as it was in the Georgian Era.

2. http://home.earthlink.net/~hogarth28/bibliog.html - A bibliographic resource for books about 18th-century Philadelphia.

18TH-CENTURY PHILADELPHIA

As originally laid out by William Penn, the city consisted of that portion of the present city situated between South and Vine Streets and Delaware and Schuylkill Rivers. Strictly speaking, the city was that portion between High (Market) Street and Dock Creek, where pioneers dug caves in the banks of the Delaware or built huts on the land higher up.

Indians were present as observers of the city's evolution or as venders of their game and venison. The Swedes and Dutch, who were the earliest settlers in the area, also brought their produce to markets in the city.

Settlements made outside of these boundaries eventually became separately incorporated and had separate governments. However, the whole group was known abroad simply as "Philadelphia."

Among these communities were Southwark and Moyamensing in the south, the Northern Liberties, Kensington, Spring Garden, and Penn District to the north, and West Philadelphia to the west—all of which were practically one town continuously built up.

There were a number of other outlying townships, villages, and settlements near the built-up town, though detached from it. They included Bridesburg, Frankford, Harrowgate, Holmesburg, the unincorporated Northern Liberties, Port Richmond, Nicetown, Rising Sun, Fox Chase, Germantown, Roxborough, Falls of Schuylkill, the unincorporated Penn township, Francisville, Hamilton Village, Mantua, Blockley, Kingsessing, and Passyunk.

Some of these places became absorbed in the extending streets of towns of which Philadelphia was composed.

Southwark, on the river front, was marked by wood-yards that supplied fuel before the days of anthracite coal, also by the sheds and yards of boat-builders and mast-makers, and by ship-builders' yards, including the United States Navy Yard. Many Southwark dwellings were inhabited by sea captains and seafaring men, along with the families of seagoing people and "watermen."

The district was also characterized by the extensive machine shops and ironworks of Merricks, Morris & Tasker, Savery, and others, as well as by the mechanical work promoted by the Navy Yard, situated at the foot of Federal Street.

The Northern Liberties also had cord-wood wharves and yards along the river front and extensive lumber yards. This district was also characterized, particularly along Second Street, by its farmers' market yards for the wholesale trade in butter, eggs, poultry, meats, vegetables, and other products of the farms of the adjacent country.

Long before the consolidation of the Northern Liberties into the city, Second Street was famous for its fine retail shops, and Third Street was the site of a large wholesale trade in groceries, provisions, and leather.

Pegg's Run and Cohocksink Creek, which flowed through the Northern Liberties, were the sites of numerous extensive tan yards.

One of the pioneer mills in Philadelphia's great industries, the Old Globe Mill, was near the line of the Northern Liberties, Germantown Avenue below Girard Avenue. The Northern Liberties embraced what are now the Eleventh, Twelfth, and part of the Sixteenth Wards of the city.

Kensington was a ship- and boat-building district, with a lot of its former inhabitants fishermen engaged in supplying the Philadelphia markets. The area embraced part of the present Sixteenth, Seventeenth, and Eighteenth Wards.

Spring Garden District was, in the old time, one of the most pleasant suburbs of Philadelphia and the principal dwelling-place of the Ancient and Honorable Fraternity of Butchers or Victuallers.

Port Richmond, occupying the Delaware River front to the north and northeast of Old Kensington, was brought into prominence by its immense coal traffic by sea.

This began to improve the unproductive land in the vicinity, for the shipping piers, the coal depots, the engine houses, workshops, offices, etc., were accompanied by a large increase in population, the erection of dwellings, great activity, and rapid progress in all respects.

In addition to all this bustling "blue-collar" activity, Philadelphia was known as the "Athens of America" because of its rich cultural life, the liberality of founder William Penn's principles, its freedom of expression, and the variety and strength of its intellectual and educational institutions and interests.

An academy that held its first classes in 1740 became the College of Philadelphia in 1755 and ultimately grew into the University of Pennsylvania. It was the only nondenominational college of the colonial period.

The arts and sciences flourished, and the public buildings of Philadelphia were the marvel of the colonies. Many fine old buildings in the Philadelphia area still bear witness to the richness of Pennsylvania's civilization in the 18th century.

Great thinkers such as Benjamin Franklin, David Rittenhouse, John Bartram, and Benjamin West achieved international renown. Newspapers and magazines flourished, as did law and medicine.

View of the Thames River, ca. 1757

18TH-CENTURY LONDON

In the words of Dr. Samuel Johnson, London's most literary and crusty defender: "You find no man, at all intellectual, who is willing to leave London. No, Sir, when a man is tired of London, he is tired of life; for there is in London all that life can afford."

In 1700 London was a series of communities spread along the Thames within easy reach of open fields. But by the end of the century, encouraged by new roads and new bridges, London had become a massive urban sprawl moving away from its origins along the Thames into rural Middlesex and Surrey.

The city had always been cosmopolitan, but was now the hub of an immense empire, with wealth coming from trade with the East and West Indies. London became filled by new immigrant communities and by new fashions in clothing, music, shopping, and theatre. Many of the hospitals, banks, and institutions that exist in London today were founded at this time. Tea-drinking was all the rage. Eighteenth-century London was two societies, based on wealth and residence.

The West End emerged as the residential and shopping center of the wealthy. Aristocrats who owned large rural estates developed them into London suburbs, using the residential square as the focal point of formally planned districts, unlike anything in older parts of London, where development was more unsystematic. Grosvenor, Bedford, Belgrave, and Russell Squares were all built around this time.

The urban palaces of the aristocracy stood shoulder to shoulder around the formal squares that came to characterize Westminster. Chains, iron railings, and padlocks segregated the rich from their neighbors. At the same time the back streets and mews that filled the areas between the squares retained a diverse community of artisans, service workers, and paupers.

New types of street lighting, paving, and water supply grew in the same pattern, with remarkably high standards to be found in the West End and in those parts of the city rebuilt after the Great Fire, and equally remarkably low standards in other areas. In some areas ground water from public wells was still the only source, and mud still filled the unimproved roads for much of the year. At the end of the century, the building of the huge, enclosed docks east of the Tower only served to emphasize the relative squalor of the surrounding communities.

The other London was the East End, with its dockyards, and the islands of poverty scattered through the rest of the city. Child mortality, disease, and crime were prevalent in these areas. The desperate situation was worsened by high consumption of gin. Social violence, crime, and major demonstrations were common, especially during the early reign of George III.

Up until at least the passage of the London Building Act of 1774, many suburban developments were haphazard and of poor quality, the work of speculators—poor carpenters and bricklayers, using even poorer materials. During periodic depressions in the building industry, houses put up in hope of attracting middling sort and rich occupants were let out room by room to the very poor. Collapses were common, with whole families occasionally crushed in their beds.

"Gin Lane" by William Hogarth, ca. 1700s

To the East and North of the City, the less fortunate of London suffered poor housing and poor infrastructure, made tolerable only by the demand for casual labor on the quays and wharves and in the service industries of the city.

Notable during this period were the riots led by John Wilkes in the late 1760s, in which he called for freedom of the press and political reforms, and the Gordon Riots of 1780, headed by Protestant leader Lord George Gordon against pro-Catholic legislation.

Cockfighting in 1700s London

BENJAMIN FRANKLIN: THE LONDON YEARS

Ben Franklin made several trips to London, both on his own and later as a representative of several American colonies.

After a quarrel with his brother in 1723, Franklin left Boston for Philadelphia, where he again worked in the printing industry. He established a friendship with the Pennsylvania governor, Sir William Keith, and at Keith's suggestion, Franklin decided to go into business for himself.

Keith offered to arrange letters of credit and introduction for Franklin's trip to London to purchase equipment. Unfortunately, Keith proved unreliable, repeatedly putting Franklin off when he called to collect several letters of reference that he had promised the young man.

Finally, on Nov. 5, 1724, armed with the personal assurances of Keith's secretary that these letters would be given him aboard ship, Franklin sailed for England. The weather was rough; however, Franklin and his fellow passengers, including his best friend, a poet named James Read, made the best of their situation.

Unfortunately, when Franklin arrived in London and was allowed to examine the mails from Pennsylvania, there was nothing addressed to him. Several inquiries by Franklin soon showed that Keith was the sort of man who promised much and delivered little. As Franklin said of Keith in later life, "He wished to please everybody, and having little to give, he gave expectations."

For the time being, this left Franklin in London little more than the clothes on his back, no means of support, and only a hard lesson in life to show for his trouble. However, he quickly found cheap lodgings and then employment in two of London's largest printing houses, first Samuel Palmer's and later John Watt's establishments. After two years he had earned enough money to return to America. He also earned enough to help out his friend Read from time to time.

The experience proved enjoyable enough over all, marred only when Read asked his friend to look after the lady he had been courting, a task which Franklin performed a little too well. Read broke off their friendship and proclaimed that under the circumstances he felt it unnecessary to repay the money he owed his former companion.

During Franklin's time at Palmer's, he helped to publish a work by one William Wollaston, "The Religion of Nature Delineated," which maintained that religious truth was to be found through the studies of nature and science as opposed to divine revelation.

Franklin was in overall agreement, but felt Wollaston was wrong in part, and so he wrote "A Dissertation on Liberty and Necessity, Pleasure and Pain" in 1725. In this work, he maintained that because God is good, all-wise, and powerful, "everything that exists or happens is with His consent." Therefore, "What He consents to must be good, because He is good; therefore evil does not exist." In addition, happiness and unhappiness, pleasure and pain are in proportion, neither can exist without the other.

Later on, Franklin grew disenchanted with his early efforts at philosophical speculation and burned as many copies of the work as he could find.

After working at Palmer's printing house for a year, Franklin moved to the larger establishment of John Watt's.

There he became known as the "Water American" for his preference in drinking hot-water gruel with bread, as opposed to the pints of thin ale that his fellow printers drank to sustain them. Still, Franklin made friends as his frugality enabled him at times to loan money to his associates after they drank up their weekly pay.

Things became a bit rocky when Franklin refused to pay a five shilling "initiation fee" upon his promotion to the composition room, a more skilled area of the business. However, after three weeks of pranks and other pressures, he submitted and paid up, a move that restored his popularity and reputation.

In his off hours, Franklin attended literary roundtables and sought out introductions to prominent people, including one Sir Hans Sloane, secretary to the Royal Society. Franklin sold him an asbestos purse that he had brought from America. He also found a bookseller who agreed to let him borrow books.

Franklin was also an avid swimmer, and in his youth had invented paddles and flippers to help him in the water. He studied the techniques described in one of the earliest books on the subject, *The Art of Swimming,* by the Frenchman Melchisedec Thevenot, including the breast stroke, which he refined. Franklin taught a number of his friends to swim and was invited by one of them to form a swimming school. But he eventually decided to return to America with a friend, a Quaker merchant named Denham, and work for Denham as a clerk. They left together in July 1726.

After Franklin's return to Philadelphia, he managed his business so well that he was able to retire at the age of forty-

INTERNATIONAL SWIMMING HALL OF FAME CITATION:

Franklin, Benjamin (1968)
Contributor, USA

Benjamin Franklin was a competent swim coach and teacher; he advised on water safety, lifeboat rescue escape from shipwrecks, and the advisability of universal learn-to-swim classes.

One of the United States' first "ornamental swimmers," on a Thames River excursion in 1726, he swam from Chelsea to Blackfriars (3½ miles) "performing on the way many feats of activity, both upon and under water, that surprised and pleased those to whom they were novelties."

Presented to
Benjamin Franklin
Outstanding Contributor
In recognition of his nomination and unanimous election to the
Swimming Hall of Fame
Where his world recognized achievements attendant to swimming immortality shall be permanently enshrined.
Presented December 28, 1968 before 3000 of his swimming peers at Fort Lauderdale, Florida by the authority vested in me from the swimming groups universally represented in the Swimming Hall of Fame, Incorporated.

President

Benjamin Franklin Returns

Benjamin Franklin offering advice on success in printing to the workers at Watt's print shop on his second visit to London.

two, with income of 500 pounds a year (which was a lot for the time), and devote his energies to science and politics. He maintained a lively correspondence with scientists and scholars on both sides of the Atlantic.

In 1748 Franklin sold his printing business and, in 1750, was elected to the Pennsylvania Assembly, in which he served until 1764.

He was appointed deputy postmaster general for the colonies in 1753, and in 1754 he was the delegate from Pennsylvania to the intercolonial congress that met at Albany to consider methods of dealing with the threatened French and Indian War (1754-1763).

His "Albany Plan," in many ways prophetic of the 1787 U.S. Constitution, provided for local independence within a framework of colonial union, but was too far in advance of public thinking to obtain ratification. Franklin believed that the adoption of this plan would have averted the American Revolution.

When the French and Indian War broke out, Franklin procured horses, wagons, and supplies for the British commander General Edward Braddock by pledging his own credit to the Pennsylvania farmers, who thereupon furnished the necessary equipment.

The proprietors of Pennsylvania Colony, descendants of the Quaker leader William Penn, in conformity with their religious opposition to war, refused to allow their landholdings to be taxed for the prosecution of the war.

Franklin returned to London in 1757 to represent the Colony of Pennsylvania as its Agent (an ambassador of sorts). In practice, he represented the colonial assembly in its efforts to get the king to lift its status as a proprietary colony.

During his stay, Franklin lodged with a widow named Margaret Stevenson, whom he also escorted to various events in the city, though their relationship seems to have been largely on the side of friendship. He was also very close to her daughter Mary, also known as Polly, with whom he frequently spoke or exchanged letters. In fact, she was at his bedside when he died, thirty-three years after they first met.

Franklin remained in England for the next five years, in the center of London's intellectual and literary scene. He avoided much of the aristocracy, preferring to be with people with minds as lively and as enquiring as his own.

Never a snob, Franklin made a visit to one of the press rooms where he had worked during his previous stay, treating all there to buckets of beer and toasting "the success of printing."

During this time, Franklin was elected the first American member of the Royal Society, through which he secured the friendship of many prominent Londoners.

In 1761, Franklin visited Holland, noting that the Dutch were not so strict about religion as the Americans. He was interested to see that the Dutch would even attend plays on Sunday, concluding this "would almost make one suspect that the Deity is not so angry at that offense as a New England justice."

Returning to England for the coronation of George III in September of that year, Franklin had hopes the new king would help his colonies in their quarrels with their proprietors.

He advanced the view that continued harmony between the colonies and the mother country depended on allowing them to expand into Canada, ensuring them political parity with England and providing a good market for British goods.

"While the government is mild and just, while important civil and religious rights are secure, such subjects will be dutiful and obedient," he said, but also noted that treating the colonies as second-class citizens and markets to be exploited could "provoke the future independence" of the colonies.

Franklin returned to Pennsylvania in November 1762. In early 1763 he toured New Jersey, New York, and New England inspecting post offices in his role as Postmaster General.

As an agent of the Pennsylvania Assembly, Franklin, with son William in tow, returned to England in 1764. Franklin expected a short visit, but it lasted ten years, until the start of the American Revolution. He was sent to help defeat the unpopular Stamp Act.

This act, by which the Crown intended to recover some of the expenses of the French and Indian War, required colonists to pay for a stamp on newspapers, books, almanacs, legal documents, and even decks of cards.

It was the first time the British government ever proposed an internal tax on the colonies and was vigorously opposed by many Americans, a depth of feeling that

King George III

George III (1738-1820), in full, George William Frederick, was King of England from 1760 to 1820. He was the first of the House of Hanover to be born in England. His early reign was trouble-filled, marked by difficulties with government ministers and the loss of the American colonies. He was deeply religious and tried to be a conscientious ruler to his subjects, which earned him respect over the years. Bouts of recurring mental illness affected him from 1788 on. Blindness and permanent madness took hold in 1810, and his son ruled as Prince Regent for the ten years until King George died at 81.

Franklin may not have quite understood on the far side of the Atlantic. In any case, he attempted a reasonable approach, which backfired.

As he wrote to a friend, "We might well have hindered the sun's setting. That we could not do. But since it is down—and it may be long before it rises again—let us make as good a night of it as we can. We may still light candles."

Sadly, Franklin's reputation suffered when he misinterpreted the depth of feeling back home about the question and sought to compromise with the Crown over the matter.

But a letter-writing campaign by Franklin and others served to restore his standing. He also espoused a boycott of British imports and other transactions. He got people to write on his behalf back home, as when a prominent London Quaker named John Fothergill wrote to an American friend, "I can safely aver that Benjamin Franklin did all in his power to prevent the Stamp Act from passing. He asserted the rights and privileges of Americans with the utmost firmness."

Franklin himself wrote copiously, at least thirteen letters in a three-month period with at least two under the name "Homespun," in which he said Americans could do without British imports and make their own substitutes for the items requiring the hated stamps, even saying they could make tea from the green ears of corn.

Finally, Franklin's later appearance before the House of Commons in a staged question-and-answer appearance aided in the Act's eventual overturn. Many of the questions were scripted in advance by a government now sympathetic to the Americans and looking for a way out of the problem.

Eventually, Franklin became the unofficial spokesman of the Americans in their disputes with the Crown. He became the official agent for Georgia in 1768, New Jersey in 1769, and Massachusetts in 1770, in addition to Pennsylvania, holding all these positions simultaneously.

Also a representative of his own and other colonies, at this time Franklin believed in the British Empire and the American place in it. Sadly, he soon learned that for many in the government, including Lord Granville, the president of the King's Privy Council, that place was at a much lower level than for native-born Englishmen.

Franklin held that laws passed by the colonial assemblies were on par with the dictates of colonial governors. Granville's opinion was that "You Americans have wrong ideas of the nature of your constitution," and that the instructions of the governors were "the law of the land."

He also fell into serious dispute with the

Plaque on Benjamin Franklin's London Residence

A London County Council plaque marks the London residence of American statesman, philosopher, and scientist, Benjamin Franklin.

Penns, who held the proprietorship of Pennsylvania over the powers of the Assembly. The quarrel grew so heated that any hope of a reasonable solution became impossible.

At one point, his friend Strahan published an anonymous attack by Franklin on the Penns, calling their actions with regard to Pennsylvania as being against the interests of Britain. Another letter, signed by William but clearly prepared with his father's help, actually attacked the Penns directly.

Since his relationship to the government had so seriously broken down, Franklin and son spent some time traveling throughout England to visit the friends he had made outside of politics.

During his third stay in England, Franklin combined a social life with both diplomacy and science, interacting with such notables as the Quaker merchant and botanist Peter Collinson and the printer William Strahan, whom he had previously only known through a lengthy correspondence. Strahan was also part-owner of the London *Chronicle.*

He even had time to conduct a series of experiments with a Cambridge-based chemist named John Hadley. They studied the evaporation rates of ether and speculated that breezes don't cool people, but rather cooling is brought about by increased evaporation caused by the breeze.

A highlight of his English travels involved meeting David Hume, considered one of the greatest thinkers of all time. Hume was also the author of such works as "A Treatise of Human Nature" and "Essays Concerning Human Understanding," as well as his most famous work, the six volume "History of England."

Although they disagreed on such things as Franklin's use of words such as "unshakeable" and "colonize," he remained a great admirer of Franklin, saying "America has sent us many good things, gold, silver, sugar, tobacco, indigo. But you are the first [American] philosopher, and indeed the first great man of letters, for whom we are beholden to her."

It was during this third visit that Franklin, then sixty-five, over a two-week period in August of 1771 composed the first part of his memoirs, starting the work at the home of Jonathan Shipley, bishop of St. Asaph, a task that occupied him off and on for the next eighteen years.

Soon, however, new plans for taxing the colonies were introduced in Parliament. Franklin hadn't quite realized how angry people were back home and still sought to settle the matter with discussion. But he was increasingly divided between his devotion to his native land and his loyalty as a subject of George III of Great Britain.

Finally, in 1775, recognizing the inevitability of war, Franklin made his choice and went home. Franklin reached Philadelphia on May 5, 1775, to find that the opening engagements of the Revolution—the battles of Lexington and Concord—had already been fought.

Before beginning this lecture you may want to . . .

Read H.W. Brands' The First American, Chapter 4.

Introduction:

Despite the disappointment of his failed London trip, Franklin returned to Philadelphia determined to make it as a printer. Through a combination of hard work, business savvy, and knowledge of public desires, he soon achieved the financial and employment independence he had craved since his days as an apprentice with his brother in Boston.

Consider this . . .

1. What aspects of Franklin's personality aided him in finally establishing his print business in Philadelphia?

2. How did Franklin expand his business through his knowledge of what was popular among readers of the day?

I. **Franklin arrived back in Philadelphia full of energy and ambition but short of money.**

   A. Franklin was almost twenty when he returned to Philadelphia from London.

   1. He was full grown, of somewhat greater than average height.

   2. Broad shouldered, with thick arms from carrying all the lead type and cranking the press screw, he had all the energy in the world.

   3. He was very ambitious about plans to start his own printing business.

   4. He lacked the capital he needed to go into business on his own.

   B. He found a partner named Meredith, whose father had some money and wanted to set up his son.

   1. Meredith's money and Franklin's savvy helped the partnership land some government contracts, including one for printing paper currency.

   2. Franklin began to build a reputation as an effective printer.

   C. Meredith squandered the reputation of the press.

   1. Lazy, often drunk, he became a drag on the business.

   2. Franklin puzzled about how to relieve himself of this burden.

   3. He agreed to buy out Meredith for thirty pounds sterling, a new saddle (Meredith was heading to North Carolina), and the assumption of some debts.

II. **Full owner of his own print shop at last, Franklin established himself as a respected businessman in Philadelphia.**
   A. Now his own man, his future resting on himself alone, Franklin threw himself more than ever into his work.
      1. He cultivated clients, impressing all Philadelphia with his work habits.
      2. He came to work early.
      3. He worked long hours.
      4. He covered all aspects of the business.
   B. He purchased *The Pennsylvania Gazette* from his old employer, and recent competitor, Samuel Keimer.
      1. It was a local paper, but Franklin had larger ambitions.
         i. He reprinted news from around the colonies and the empire.
         ii. He wrote pieces he hoped would be similarly reproduced.
      2. He understood the gifts required of a good editor.
         i. "The author of a gazette (in the opinion of the learned) ought to be qualified with an extensive acquaintance with languages, a great easiness and command of writing and relating things cleanly and intelligibly, and in few words; he should be able to speak of war both by land and sea, be well acquainted with geography, with the history of the time, with the several interests of princes and states, the secrets of courts, and the manners and customs of all nations."
         ii. Franklin felt that a paper must be edifying, but it must also be "as agreeable and useful an entertainment as the nature of the thing will allow."
      3. This combination of edification and entertainment made for a popular paper.
   C. Franklin hoped to improve the tenor of life in Philadelphia with his paper, but he never forgot that printing was a business, not a political activity.
      1. He continued doing much of his own writing, including letters.
      2. He accepted a wide variety of advertising.
      3. He practiced fairness in presenting the views of others: "Printers are educated in the belief that when men differ in opinion both sides ought equally to have the advantage of being heard by the public, and that when truth and error have fair play, the former is always an overmatch of the latter. Hence they cheerfully serve all contending parties that pay them well."

III. **Franklin added to his reputation by developing *Poor Richard's Almanack*.**
   A. Always on the lookout for ways to boost readership and revenue, he recognized the popularity of almanacs.
   B. In December 1732 the *Gazette* ran a notice announcing the first publication of *Poor Richard's*.

THE PENNSYLVANIA GAZETTE

In October of 1729, Benjamin Franklin bought the Pennsylvania Gazette, a dull, poorly edited weekly newspaper. In his first editorial, Franklin told his readers "there are many who have long desired to see a good newspaper in Pennsylvania."

So he took this dull and poorly edited paper and turned it, by his own witty style and judicious selection of news, into a publication that was both entertaining and informative.

During the *Gazette's* lifetime, the paper published such important documents as the *United States Constitution*, *Declaration of Independence*, *The Federalist Papers*, and Thomas Paine's *Common Sense*.

It also published items more typical of the newspapers of the time, including short news items and reports on public events, essays, and letters from readers. However, a number of these "letters" came from Franklin himself, who used the forum to have more leeway in commentary, poke fun at rivals, offer gossip, and air his own ideas.

But Franklin was devoted to the free expression of other ideas as well. He wrote "Printers are educated in the belief that when men differ in opinion, both sides ought equally to have the advantage of being heard by the public; and that when Truth and Error have fair play, the former is always an overmatch for the latter."

He added, "It is unreasonable to imagine that printers approve of everything they print. It is likewise unreasonable what some assert, that printers ought not to print anything but what they approve; since . . . an end would thereby be put to free printing, and the world would afterwards have nothing to read but what happened to be the opinions of printers."

At the same time, Franklin's policy was to balance free expression with discretion. Or as he put it, "I myself have constantly refused to print anything that might countenance vice or promote immoral thought. . . . I might have got much money. I have also always refused to print such things as might do real injury to any person."

Ideals notwithstanding, Franklin was aware of the things that sell newspapers in his (or in modern) times—sex, sensationalism, and gossip.

He called the last a curb on the egos of important people, as well as a way to encourage virtue in people, whether out of their own goodness or the fear of public chastisement. But, mindful of his wish never to be mean, he never let the *Gazette* turn into a tabloid or scandal sheet as a modern reader might understand the term.

Instead, he sought to promote sobriety and frugality in the pages of the *Gazette*. He wrote letters using pseudonyms such as "Alice Addertounge" to illustrate the foibles of human nature. Franklin also wrote and printed letters designed to entertain and instruct.

In one of "Alice's" letters she described a disagreement with her mother, who "argued that scandal spoiled all good conversation, and I insisted without it there can be no such thing. This resulted in Alice's exile to the kitchen when visitors came to tea, however said visitors tended to drift into Alice's orbit sooner or later to hear her and her friends."

A lesson on frugality was illustrated when Franklin, in the voice of one "Anthony Afterwit," taught his free-spending wife a lesson by selling all her fancy things while she was visiting her family. He buys a spinning wheel and some knitting needs, and asks the *Gazette* to publish this news to prepare his wife for the new order of things, in the hopes that she will understand. If so, he promises to let her have a nice mirror at least.

On more serious matters, such as health and politics, Franklin remained an advocate in his paper of inoculation and published figures and statistics supporting its effectiveness.

With regard to politics, when Great Britain continued its policies of restricting development of the colonies in order to keep them as a cheap labor pool and a captive market for finished goods, Franklin wrote, "Britain should not too much restrain manufactures in her colonies. A wise and good mother will not do it. To distress is to weaken, and weakening the children weakens the whole family."

Finally, writing as Americanus on the issue of transporting convicts to the colonies, justified as a way to help them grow, Franklin responded that America should ship a load of rattlesnakes back to England in hopes the climate there would tame the reptiles. And even if not, "the rattlesnake gives warning before he attempts his mischief, which the convict does not."

POOR RICHARD'S ALMANACK

First published by Benjamin Franklin in 1732, *Poor Richard's Almanack* was a guide to both weather forecasts and a source of wise maxims. Its name echoed that of *Poor Robin's Almanack,* as published by Franklin's brother James.

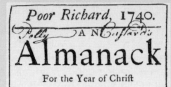

Franklin used the pseudonym Richard Saunders (also the name of a real almanac writer in England during the 17th century) in writing the text, which soon became an annual publication up until 1757 when he left for England. Response to the almanac was tremendous, and it sold as many as 10,000 issues a year.

He wrote *Poor Richard's Almanack* as a service to the American people, hoping to educate them and entice their intellectual appetites. As Richard Saunders, Franklin was given both the freedom to express his thoughts and the freedom to do so with dramatic license.

Consequently, Franklin emphasized the two qualities he found most essential to success: industry and frugality.

Franklin issued the almanac from 1732 to 1757. Long after his connection with it was in name only, *Poor Richard's* still had an enormous circulation. In 1766, for example, 141,257 copies were sold.

In later years, the sayings in the book were published as "The Way to Wealth," and it became the most famous American work of its time. Within forty years, that book went through 145 editions in seven languages. Including the present time, the book has gone through over 1,300 printings.

Franklin called his almanac a "vehicle for conveying instruction among the common folk" and so filled it with sayings intended to encourage "industry and frugality as the means of procuring wealth and thereby securing virtue."

Among these sayings were the following:

Sloth, like Rust, consumes faster than Labour wears, while the used Key is always bright.

The sleeping Fox catches no Poultry.

The general foible of mankind is the pursuit of wealth to no end.

Lost Time is never found again.

Sloth makes all Things difficult, He that riseth late, must trot all Day, and shall scarce overtake his Business at Night.

Early to Bed, and early to rise, makes a Man healthy, wealthy and wise.

He that lives upon Hope will die fasting.

There are no Gains, without Pains.

At the working Man's House Hunger looks in, but dares not enter.

Industry pays Debts, while Despair encreaseth them.

Diligence is the Mother of Good luck.

One Today is worth two Tomorrows.

Are you then your own Master, be ashamed to catch yourself idle.

Handle your Tools without Mittens; remember that the Cat in Gloves catches no Mice.

Little Strokes fell great Oaks.

I never saw an oft removed Tree, Nor yet an oft removed Family, That throve so well as those that settled be.

Keep thy Shop, and thy Shop will keep thee.

He that by the Plough would thrive, Himself must either hold or drive.

If you would be wealthy, think of Saving as well as of Getting.

Women and Wine, Game and Deceit, Make the Wealth small, and the Wants great.

What maintains one Vice, would bring up two Children.

Fools make Feasts, and wise Men eat them.

Wise Men learn by others' Harms, Fools scarcely by their own.

A Ploughman on his Legs is higher than a Gentleman on his Knees.

C. Franklin's almanac added to a useful, popular form of periodical.

   1. He included important practical information about tides, moons, and frosts.

   2. He presented astrological information for a public looking for explanations about the causes and effects of the world.

   3. He competed directly against popular almanacker Titus Leeds.

      i. "Richard Saunders" predicted the imminent death of Titus Leeds.

      ii. This encouraged an angry response from Leeds.

      iii. Franklin humorously turned the table on Leeds.

   4. Franklin added his own contributions to the almanacker's art and to American folk wisdom by filling up empty spaces on pages.

      i. His sayings, while not always original, made the pithy pithier and the pointed more provocative: "Great talkers, little doers." "Gifts burst rocks." "Hunger never saw bad bread."

      ii. He addressed the battle of the sexes: "When man and woman die, as poets sung/His heart's the last part moves, her last the tongue." "One good husband is worth two good wives, for the scarcer things are, the more they're valued."

      iii. He skewered the professions: "A countryman between two lawyers is like a fish between two cats." "Never spare the parson's wine nor the baker's pudding." "God heals, and the doctor takes the fee." "Eyes and priests bear no jests."

iv. His nom de plume allowed him to be as earthy as he wanted: "Neither a fortress nor a maidenhead will hold out long after they begin to parley." "The greatest monarch on the proudest throne is obliged to sit upon his own arse." "Force shits upon reason's back."

5. Part of the almanac's success came from Franklin's willingness to tweak himself and his fellow almanackers.

   i. "Ignorant men wonder how we astrologers foretell the weather so exactly, unless we deal with the old black Devil," Saunders told readers. In fact, the astrologer's work was far simpler than that. " 'Tis easy as pissing abed. For instance, the stargazer peeps at the heavens through a long glass; he sees perhaps Taurus, or the great bull, in a mighty chase, stamping on the floor of his house, swinging his tail about, stretching out his neck, and opening wide his mouth. 'Tis natural from these appearances to judge that this furious bull is puffing, blowing, and roaring. Distance being considered, and time allowed for all this to come down, there you have wind and thunder."

   ii. Franklin sent up the whole business of the almanacker predicting the weather in a way that got hoots in kitchens and workshops around the colony. "He spies perhaps Virgo (the Virgin). She turns her head round, as it were to see if anybody observed her. Then crouching down gently, with her hands on her knees, she looks wistfully for a while right forward. He judges rightly what she's about; and having calculated the distance and allowed time for its falling, finds that the next spring we shall have a fine April shower."

Summary: Most of the qualities later generations have come to associate Franklin with can clearly be seen in his efforts to establish himself in business in his early days in Philadelphia. In particular, his hard work and business savvy enabled him to establish a reputation as a man who could be trusted to get things done.

A cautionary jingle written by Franklin hung over the entry door to his Philadelphia print shop:

All ye who come this curious art to see,
To handle anything must cautious be,
Lest, by a slight touch, ere you are aware,
A mischief may be done you can't repair.
Lo! This advice we give to every stranger,
Look on, and welcome; but to touch there's danger!

FOR GREATER UNDERSTANDING

Consider

1. What was Franklin's greatest strength as a businessman?
2. What role should a newspaper play in improving the lives of the people in the area it serves?

Suggested Reading

Franklin, Benjamin. Poor Richard's Almanack. New York: Peter Pauper Press, 1984.

Websites to Visit

1. http://www.ushistory.org/franklin/index.htm - Within this site is general information on Franklin as well as The Pennsylvania Gazette, a Tour of Franklin's Philadelphia, photos, and more.

2. http://www.earlyamerica.com/earlyamerica/past/past.html - An image of The Pennsylvania Gazette from January 2, 1750, is featured.

3. http://pennsylvaniagazette.blogspot.com/ - The contemporary version of The Pennsylvania Gazette. It has a brief history of the newspaper and a modern archive of recent issues.

4. http://www.sims.berkeley.edu/academics/courses/is182/s01/second53. html - Facsimilies of Poor Richard's Almanack from various years.

5. http://www.geocities.com/peterroberts.geo/BFrWr.html - Click on "Poor Richard's Almanack." This will display a list of images of pages from over twenty original Almanacks. They are very readable on screen.

Before beginning this lecture you may want to . . .

Read H.W. Brands' The First American, Chapters 4-5.

Introduction:

One of Franklin's most intriguing personal "experiments" had to do with his efforts at creating a type of personal virtue for himself. He felt that through a rational, logical approach, he could turn himself into a moral person without the need for formal religion.

Consider this . . .

1. What role did religion play in shaping Franklin's moral philosophy?

2. What basic "commandments" did Franklin believe were important to conducting a happy, productive life?

I. **Franklin felt moral and ethical beliefs did not need to be tied to formal religion.**

A. Having rejected the Puritan theology of his boyhood, Franklin was left to find a basis for good behavior in himself and others.

1. He rejected the theology of predestination and other Puritan beliefs.

2. He retained much of Puritan ethics, especially as applied to work.

3. Justifying the contradictions between what he believed religiously and what he was unable to reconcile with his personal, more enlightened vision of the world became an important ongoing conflict in Franklin's life.

B. Franklin's underlying philosophy did not believe in sin, original or otherwise.

1. He did not believe in disembodied evil.

2. He did not feel there was a "dark side" of humanity.

C. Franklin also had difficulty believing in the orthodox vision of revelation.

1. He did not believe the Bible and other holy books were "divinely inspired."

2. He gradually came to view these works as a summary of human wisdom.

3. This led to his fundamental conclusion about the link between revelation and action: "I entertained an opinion that though certain actions might not be bad because they were forbidden by it [revelation], or good because it commanded them, yet probably those actions might be forbidden because they were bad for us, or commanded because they were beneficial to us."

Mark Twain at Home in Bed

TWAIN ON FRANKLIN

"If it had not been for him, with his incendiary 'Early to bed and early to rise,' and all that sort of foolishness, I wouldn't have been so harried and worried and raked out of bed at such unseemly hours when I was young. The late Franklin was well enough in his way; but it would have looked more dignified in him to have gone on making candles and letting other people get up when they wanted to."

—Letter from Mark Twain, San Francisco, California, July 25, 1869

    4. In other words, man—not God—was the measure of morality, so men could control their own actions and behave "morally" for their own personal happiness.

    5. This philosophy marks Franklin as one of the first American humanists.

II. **Franklin decided to perform an experiment on himself to see if he could cultivate virtue through personal attitude rather than through divine intervention.**

A. He considered what caused people to err into immorality.

    1. He concluded that people had an insufficient understanding of the costs and benefits of their behavior.

       i. They had difficulty distinguishing short-term benefits from long-term benefits.

       ii. They couldn't see the distinction between personal benefits and community benefits.

    2. He perceived that people also acted against their larger greater pleasure simply out of bad habit: laziness, forgetfulness, uncharitableness.

B. Since he saw reasons for slipping into immoral behavior, Franklin deter-mined that people could become virtuous by inculcating good habits.

   1. By practicing order, a person could become orderly—until it no longer took any effort.

   2. Showing moderation in food and drink required tuning one's tastes to moderation.

   3. Diligence would pay off in material success, which would reinforce further diligence.

C. Franklin's experiment began with four "commandments" for conducting his life.

   1. They dealt with both the state of his soul and the state of his daily life.

   2. His code of ethics was devised to make life on Earth happier, not out of concern for any heavenly afterlife.

   3. This was an eminently practical code of behavior, well suited to one starting out in life on his own.

   4. The "commandments" reflected Franklin's practicality.

      i. Frugality to eliminate burdens of debt

      ii. Truth to reflect rationality

      iii. Industry to lead to success in business

      iv. Tact and kindness in dealing with others

D. Franklin's "experiment" continued with an outline of what he saw as twelve cardinal virtues that emphasize traits that lead to success.

E. Franklin decided the best way to cultivate these virtues was to keep a scorecard: a tablet with rows and columns for marking down his failures during the course of a week to make good behavior habitual.

III. **To Franklin's surprise, virtue proved elusive.**

A. His time wasn't his own. Thus, order came hard.

B. His own gifts made virtue less valuable to him personally than it might have been to another person.

C. Success one week didn't carry over automatically to the next: tempta-tion was never absent.

D. He was concerned that people would consider him a prig.

E. He rationalized falling off the wagon by considering it better to have tried and failed than to not have tried at all.

F. But he added that the effort wasn't a waste of time. "As those who aim at perfect writing by imitating the engraved copies, though they never reach the wished for excellence of those copies, their hand is mended by the endeavour."

Summary: Franklin's efforts to create a moral code of behavior for himself reflected the growing importance of the enlightenment in shaping individual thoughts at that time. Rather than becoming concerned by his failure to achieve success in shaping this philosophy on himself, he looked upon the entire experience as an opportunity to increase the human store of knowledge.

FOR GREATER UNDERSTANDING

Consider

1. Does an individual's philosophy come primarily from temperament or from teaching?

2. What virtues or commandments do you feel are essential to an effective moral code?

Suggested Reading

Franklin, Benjamin. Autobiography of Benjamin Franklin and Other Writings. New York: Penguin USA, 1989.

Franklin, Benjamin. Benjamin Franklin's the Art of Virtue: His Formula for Successful Living, 3rd Edition. Battle Creek, MI: Acorn Publishing, 1996.

Websites to Visit

1. http://www.crummy.com/articles/the_late_benjamin_franklin.shtml - Contains the text of Mark Twain's essay, "The Late Benjamin Franklin," which appeared in *The Galaxy* magazine, July 1870.

2. http://www.jsonline.com/lifestyle/advice/jun02/55259.asp - A short article from the *Milwaukee Journal Sentinel* entitled "Benjamin Franklin's virtues are worth adopting today," dated June 2002.

Editor's note: A general search of the Internet using the following words and phrases resulted in 12,500 listings: "Benjamin Franklin" and "Virtues."

D.H. LAWRENCE ON FRANKLIN'S "13 VIRTUES"

The English writer D.H. Lawrence didn't care for Benjamin Franklin "fencing off" the soul of man. Below is an excerpt from Lawrence's response to Franklin's "13 Virtues."

"Who knows what will come out of the soul of man? The soul of man is a dark vast forest, with wild life in it. Think of Benjamin fencing it off!

Oh, but Benjamin fenced a little tract that he called the soul of man, and proceeded to get it into cultivation. Providence, forsooth! And they think that bit of barbed wire is going to keep us in pound for ever? More fools they.

This is Benjamin's barbed wire fence. He made himself a list of virtues, which he trotted inside like a grey nag in a paddock.

1. TEMPERANCE
   Eat not to fulness; drink not to elevation.

2. SILENCE
   Speak not but what may benefit others or yourself; avoid trifling conversation.

3. ORDER
   Let all your things have their places; let each part of your business have its time.

4. RESOLUTION
   Resolve to perform what you ought; perform without fail what you resolve.

5. FRUGALITY
   Make no expense but to do good to others or yourself; i.e., waste nothing.

6. INDUSTRY
   Lose no time, be always employed in something useful; cut off all unnecessary action.

7. SINCERITY
   Use no hurtful deceit; think innocently and justly, and, if you speak, speak accordingly.

8. JUSTICE
   Wrong none by doing injuries, or omitting the benefits that are your duty.

9. MODERATION
   Avoid extremes, forbear resenting injuries as much as you think they deserve.

10. CLEANLINESS
    Tolerate no uncleanliness in body, clothes, or habitation.

11. TRANQUILITY
    Be not disturbed at trifles, or at accidents common or unavoidable.

12. CHASTITY
    Rarely use venery but for health and offspring, never to dulness, weakness, or the injury of your own or another's peace or reputation.

13. HUMILITY
    Imitate Jesus and Socrates.

A Quaker friend told Franklin that he, Benjamin, was generally considered proud, so Benjamin put in the Humility touch as an afterthought. The amusing part is the sort of humility it displays. 'Imitate Jesus and Socrates,' and mind you don't outshine either of these two. One can just imagine Socrates and Alcibiades roaring in their cups over Philadelphian Benjamin, and Jesus looking at him a little puzzled, and murmuring: 'Aren't you wise in your own conceit, Ben?'

'Henceforth be masterless,' retorts Ben. 'Be ye each one his own master unto himself, and don't let even the Lord put His spoke in.' 'Each man his own master' is but a puffing up of masterlessness.

Well, the first of Americans practiced this enticing list with assiduity, setting a national example. He had the virtues in columns, and gave himself good and bad marks according as he thought his behaviour deserved. Pity these conduct charts are lost to us. He only remarks that Order was his stumbling block. He could not learn to be neat and tidy.

Isn't it nice to have nothing worse to confess?

He was a little model, was Benjamin. Doctor Franklin. Snuff-coloured little man! Immortal soul and all!

. . . I admire him. I admire his sturdy courage first of all, then his sagacity, then his glimpsing into the thunders of electricity, then his common-sense humour. All the qualities of a great man, and never more than a great citizen. Middle-sized, sturdy, snuff-coloured Doctor Franklin, one of the soundest citizens that ever trod or 'used venery.'

I do not like him.

. . .Then for a 'list.' It is rather fun to play at Benjamin.

1. TEMPERANCE
   Eat and carouse with Bacchus, or munch dry bread with Jesus, but don't sit down without one of the gods.

2. SILENCE
   Be still when you have nothing to say; when genuine passion moves you, say what you've got to say, and say it hot.

3. ORDER
   Know that you are responsible to the gods inside you and to the men in whom the gods are manifest. Recognize your superiors and your inferiors, according to the gods. This is the root of all order.

4. RESOLUTION
   Resolve to abide by your own deepest promptings, and to sacrifice the smaller thing to the greater. Kill when you must, and be killed the same: the must coming from the gods inside you, or from the men in whom you recognize the Holy Ghost.

5. FRUGALITY
   Demand nothing; accept what you see fit. Don't waste your pride or squander your emotion.

6. INDUSTRY
   Lose no time with ideals; serve the Holy Ghost; never serve mankind.

7. SINCERITY
   To be sincere is to remember that I am I, and that the other man is not me.

8. JUSTICE
   The only justice is to follow the sincere intuition of the soul, angry or gentle. Anger is just, and pity is just, but judgement is never just.

9. MODERATION
   Beware of absolutes. There are many gods.

10. CLEANLINESS
    Don't be too clean. It impoverishes the blood.

11. TRANQUILITY
    The soul has many motions, many gods come and go. Try and find your deepest issue, in every confusion, and abide by that. Obey the man in whom you recognize the Holy Ghost; command when your honour comes to command.

12. CHASTITY
    Never 'use' venery at all. Follow your passional impulse, if it be answered in the other being; but never have any motive in mind, neither offspring nor health nor even pleasure, nor even service. Only know that 'venery' is of the great gods. An offering-up of your-self to the very great gods, the dark ones, and nothing else.

13. HUMILITY
    See all men and women according to the Holy Ghost that is within them. Never yield before the barren.

There's my list. I have been trying dimly to realize it for a long time, and only America and old Benjamin have at last goaded me into trying to formulate it."

— From *Studies in Classic American Literature*, D.H. Lawrence

Before beginning this lecture you may want to . . .

Read H.W. Brands' The First American, Chapter 6.

Introduction:

One of the most attractive of Franklin's personality characteristics was the way in which his character continued to evolve during the course of his long life—right until his death. In conjunction with his efforts to make himself a better person, Franklin realized the importance of his environment. His efforts to improve the community of Philadelphia reflected a growing American attitude for creating an environment that allowed individuals to excel in their chosen activities.

Consider this . . .

1. How did Franklin's attempts at self-improvement prove advantageous to the citizens of Philadelphia?

2. If his life at home had been more enjoyable, would Franklin have been less of a success in business?

I. **Franklin had an ability to align his own self-interest with the interests of the community in which he lived.**

A. Franklin's life contained two abiding questions.

1. Who am I?

2. Where do I fit?

B. Even while trying—and failing—to achieve individual perfection, Franklin pursued initiatives designed to improve the community in which he lived.

1. When Boston could not meet the demands he placed upon it, he moved from there at age seventeen.

2. At this stage of his life, by making Philadelphia a better place to live, he made the community a fit place for him to ensure his own happiness.

3. The fit between Franklin and Philadelphia would last for approximately forty years.

C. Making a city into a proper environment for a happy and moral life wasn't an easy task, as Franklin's conception of congeniality changed over time.

1. In 1723, he had been happy for any place willing to take him in and not ask questions about where he was from and why he had left there.

2. As he became successful in business, his horizons began to broaden, and he looked for intellectual challenges he hadn't considered pressing before.

II. **Franklin looked in the community for the things he did not find at home.**

A. His marriage was affectionate, but not really a model of domestic bliss.

1. He met Deborah on his first day in Philadelphia.

2. He got to know Deborah when he took a room at her father's house.

3. A gradual understanding of a future marriage grew within the family.

   i. Her mother wanted him to make his way in business first.

   ii. Franklin's trip to London led to negligence in his relationship with Debbie.

   iii. He became distracted by "the low women of London."

   iv. Not knowing when he would return, Debbie married another man.

   v. Franklin did not much care.

   vi. Debbie was abandoned by her husband.

   vii. Though she couldn't get a divorce, she reconnected with Franklin.

   viii. Not knowing whether she was legally married, Franklin and Debbie became common-law husband and wife.

   ix. Sometime during his courtship of Debbie Read, Franklin became the father of William, by another woman.

   x. Debbie took on William as her stepson.

B. Though she was a hard-working partner, Debbie's ambitions didn't extend much beyond Market Street.

1. Franklin's ambitions continued to grow.

2. He became a man about town, then about the colonies, while Debbie remained the simple, uneducated girl she had always been.

Image Courtesy of the American Philosophical Society

Deborah Read Franklin by Benjamin Wilson, ca.1759

COMMON LAW MARRIAGE

In the United States roughly half of all newlyweds have lived together before marriage, which in some jurisdictions is legally recognized as common law marriage. This means that couples are considered married if they have lived together for a certain length of time.

In order to have a valid common law marriage, the couple must do all of the following:

• Live together for a significant period of time (not defined in any state)

• Hold themselves out as a married couple—typically this means using the same last name, referring to the other as "my husband" or "my wife" and filing a joint tax return

• Intend to be married

When a common law marriage exists, the spouses receive the same legal treatment given to formally married couples, including the requirement that they go through a legal divorce to end the marriage.

C. Trouble between Debbie and William put a strain on their marriage.

D. Their first son's death cast a shadow over the household.

1. For more than a decade Debbie feared she would not see a child of her own survive.

2. The birth of daughter Sarah in 1743 eased some problems at home.

3. The presence of William—now a teenager—kept tensions high.

III. **Not completely happy with the situation at home, Franklin became dedicated to improving the city of Philadelphia.**

A. Franklin was a constant improver. He aimed to improve himself and his surroundings.

B. The Junto, a group of young men in positions comparable to Franklin, met on Friday evenings in a local tavern.

1. They considered issues of the day.

2. They worked to improve themselves and their community.

3. They networked with other businessmen.

4. The group served as a combination book club and Rotary Club.

   i. Discussed assigned readings

   ii. Wrote essays on assigned topics

C. Franklin helped establish the Library Company, which became the first lending library in America.

D. He was a founding member of the Union Fire Company.

1. Practiced fighting fires

2. Purchased equipment needed to effectively keep fires from spreading

3. Pledged to fight looting

E. His interest in science and all aspects of human endeavor led him to establish the American Philosophical Society.

1. The group coordinated activities of philosophers around the country.

2. They provided a forum to share information with other members.

F. He helped found the Academy of Philadelphia (forerunner of the University of Pennsylvania).

1. He wanted a local, non-sectarian option to educate young Americans.

2. He was concerned with preventing a "brain drain" of best young citizens to foreign countries.

G. He invented the "Franklin stove," but refused to patent it, so everyone could benefit.

Summary: By the mid-1740s, after Franklin had been in Philadelphia a little more than twenty years, he was generally considered the leading citizen of the city and the province. As James Logan, a lion of the Philadelphia establishment, said of Franklin's latest efforts on behalf of his adopted city, "He is the principal mover and very soul of the whole."

THE LIBRARY COMPANY
OF PHILADELPHIA

Franklin's subscription library was the first library of its kind in America. There were other libraries in the colonies, which he used whenever possible, but they were private libraries, not meant for general public use.

It began on July 1, 1731. Benjamin Franklin and fellow members of a society they called the Junto drew up "Articles of Agreement" to found a library that would provide them with written materials that would, among other things, provide authoritative resources to resolve any disagreement.

The Junto was a discussion group of young men seeking social, economic, intellectual, and political advancement.

Franklin recruited subscribers who would pay dues for the right to borrow books, imported for the most part from London. These subscribers included ordinary tradesmen and other average citizens, but building the library enabled Franklin to enter some of the more rarified levels of Philadelphia society in order to garner support. Fifty subscribers invested forty shillings each and promised to pay ten shillings a year thereafter to buy books and maintain a shareholder's library.

A seal, or library emblem, was decided upon with the device: "Two Books open, Each encompass'd with Glory, or Beams of Light, between which water streaming from above into an Urn below, thence issues at many Vents into lesser Urns, and Motto, circumscribing the whole, 'Communiter Bona profundere Deum est.'" ("To pour fourth benefits for the common good is divine.")

Library Hall
in Philadelphia

A statue of Benjamin Franklin stands in a niche of the door of Library Hall in Philadelphia. The hall is an exact reconstruction of the original Library Company of Philadelphia.

The terms of the library were that each borrower might take one book at a time, leaving a promissory note to cover the cost of the book, just in case. Upon each book's return, the note would be voided.

During the process of the library's creation, Franklin kept as low a profile as possible, having learned that people can be reluctant to support "any useful project that might be supposed to raise one's reputation."

So to accomplish his goal, "I therefore put myself as much as I could out of sight and stated it as a scheme of a number of friends, who had requested me to go about and propose it to such as they thought lovers of reading."

In the process, Franklin learned people eventually give credit to the right person as long as he doesn't make a point of claiming it.

Of the initial forty-five books in the library, there were eight on history, nine on science, eight on politics, and two classics. The rest were reference works.

Suitably settled, the library could turn its attention to making known its holdings. Although broadsheet catalogues of the Library Company's books may have been issued in 1733 and 1735, no copy of either survives.

An existing small octavo of fifty-six pages, printed by Franklin and issued in 1741 (pictured at right), lists the 375 titles then in the library. As 18th-century catalogues go it was a good one, the first American library catalogue to give titles at some length as well as place and date of publication.

Franklin wrote "A Short Account of the Library" to fill a final blank page. No waste, no want. Franklin noted that the library was open Saturday afternoons from four until eight o'clock. Members could borrow books freely and without charge. Nonmembers could borrow books by depositing their value as security "and paying a small Acknowledgment for the Reading." In the early days this latter fee was apparently either never collected or was waived.

Some of the earliest contributions came in in February 1733, when the original librarian Louis Timothy, Secretary Joseph Breintnall, and Franklin presented a number of volumes, including *A Collection of Several Pieces* by John Locke; *Logic: or, the Art of Thinking* by the Port Royalists Arnauld and Nicole, which Franklin in his autobiography said he had read at the age of sixteen; Plutarch's *Morals in the Translation of Philemon Holland;* Lewis Roberts' *Merchants Mappe of Commerce,* and others.

T.JH E
GENERAL MAGAZINE,
A N D
Historical Chronicle,
For all the *British* Plantations in *America.*
[To be Continued Monthly.]

JANUARY, 1741.

VOL. I.

PHILADELPHIA:
Printed and Sold by B. FRANKLIN.

The front page of "The General Magazine and Historical Chronicle For all the British Plantations in America," printed and sold by Benjamin Franklin. It is the first library journal published in America and bears the Crest of the Prince of Wales in the center.

A bit later William Rawle added a set of Spenser's works to the collection and Francis Richardson gave several volumes, among them Francis Bacon's *Sylva Sylvarum.*

Among those who guided the destinies of the Library Company in the years before the Revolution were the silversmith Philip Syng, Dr. Thomas Cadwalader, the schoolmaster Francis Alison, the builder-architect Samuel Rhoads, secretary Richard Peters of the Governor's Council, and a bit later the merchant-patriot Charles Thomson and John Dickinson, the "Pennsylvania Farmer." On May 9, 1769, Sarah Wistar became the first woman to be voted a share.

An unsolicited and greatly appreciated gift of £34 sterling arrived in the summer of 1738 from Walter Sydserfe, Scottish-born physician and planter of Antigua, who had heard of the establishment of the library from John Sober, one of its original directors.

The idea of the library caught on with the other colonies. In Franklin's words, "These libraries have improved the general conversation of the Americans, and made the common tradesmen and farmers as intelligent as most gentlemen from other countries."

The Library Company flourished because it adopted a purchasing policy responsive to the needs of its intellectually alert, economically ambitious, but non-elite membership.

By the time the library issued its earliest surviving printed catalogue of 1741, the general mix of its collection had been established for over a century.

Excluding gifts, historical works broadly defined accounted for approximately one-third of the total holdings, including geographical books and accounts of voyages and travels.

Literature—plays and poems mostly—comprised a little more than twenty percent, approximately the same proportion as science. Theology accounted for only a tenth of the titles.

The library soon became not only an increasing collection of books but also a full-fledged cabinet of curiosities in the Renaissance mode. Donors deposited in its rooms antique coins, fossils, fauna pickled in spirits, unusual geological specimens, tanned skins, and other oddities. In accordance with its role as an all-embracing cultural institution, the Library Company also participated in the increasingly popular scientific experimentation of its day, including some of the electrical experiments that made Franklin so famous.

In 1752 a surprise gift of a collection of Roman coins came from Charles Gray, a Tory member of Parliament from Colchester, who later voted against the repeal of the Stamp Act.

Two years later Charles Swaine deposited in the Library Company's room some tools and Eskimo parkas that were the only tangible fruits of the aborted Philadelphia-financed expedition to seek a Northwest Passage.

In the care of Francis Hopkinson, Benjamin West sent over the hand of a mummified Egyptian princess.

The institution's microscope and telescope were frequently requested for use by various scientific investigators. The latter at one time had to be sent

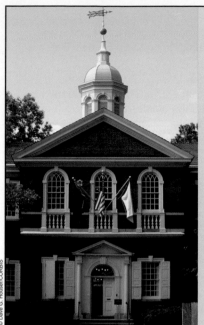

**Carpenter's Hall
Philadelphia**

For a time, the Library Company was located on the second floor of Carpenter's Hall.

to the London instrument-maker James Short to be repaired, and in 1769 it was used by Owen Biddle to observe the transit of Venus from Cape Henlopen.

In 1772 the library having "become large & valuable, a Source of Instruction to Individuals and conducive of Reputation to the Public," and much too crowded in its State House rooms, the directors petitioned the Pennsylvania Assembly for permission to build on the State House Square. The request was turned down. After much consideration and no alleviation of the space problem, agreement was reached with the Carpenters' Company in 1773 to rent the second floor of their new hall off Chestnut Street near Fourth. "The Books (inclosed within Wire Lattices) are kept in one large Room," Franklin then in London was informed, "and in another handsome Appartment the [scientific] Apparatus is deposited and the Directors meet."

It was a historic move. On September 5, 1774, the First Continental Congress met on the first floor of Carpenter's Hall. John Adams reported that the site committee had taken "a View of the Room, and of the Chamber where is an excellent Library."

In anticipation of the meeting the Library Company had ordered that "the Librarian furnish the Gentlemen who are to meet in Congress in this City with the use of such Books as they may have occasion for during their sitting taking a Receipt for them."

The first day it met Congress recorded the credentials of the delegates. On the second day it formally expressed its thanks for the Library Company's courtesy.

The offer of the use of the collections was renewed when the Second Continental Congress met the following spring, and again when the delegates to the Constitutional Convention met in 1787. In fact, for a quarter century, from 1774 until the national capital was established in Washington, D.C., in 1800, the Library Company, long the most important book resource for colonial Philadelphians, served as the de facto Library of Congress before there was one *de jure*.

Today, the Library Company of Philadelphia is a non-profit independent research library with collections documenting every aspect of the history and background of American culture from the colonial period to the end of the 19th century. Its holdings include about 500,000 printed volumes in a wide variety of formats; 75,000 images; 160,000 manuscripts; and a small, distinguished collection of early Americana.

FOR GREATER UNDERSTANDING

Consider

1. What role does community play in the life of individual citizens?

2. How much of Franklin's civic energies can be attributed to disappointment in his personal and married life?

Suggested Reading

Anderson, Douglas. Radical Enlightenments of Benjamin Franklin. Baltimore, MD: Johns Hopkins University Press, 2000.

Boorstin, Daniel J. The Americans: The Colonial Experience, Vol. 1. New York: Random House, 1972.

Taylor, Dale. Everyday Life in Colonial America. Cincinnati, OH: F & W Publications, Inc., 2002.

Websites to Visit

1. http://www.historycarper.com/resources/twobf1/contents.htm - This site has several volumes of the writings of Benjamin Franklin. The selections include his public and private writings as well as those done under pseudonyms.

2. http://www.historycarper.com/resources/twobf2/apologue.htm - This page of the site listed above gives the full text of Franklin's letter to a young man on both the benefits of marriage and of a mistress.

Before beginning this lecture you may want to . . .

Read H.W. Brands' The First American, Chapter 6.

Introduction:

The activities that won Franklin his world reputation came in the area of science and philosophical pursuit. After retiring from the business world at a relatively young age, he became the world's leading authority on electricity, eventually winning his generation's equivalent of today's Nobel Prize.

Consider this . . .

1. If there had been no American Revolution, which of the Founding Fathers would still be remembered today?

2. Why did Franklin focus his scientific inquiries in the area of electricity?

I. **Franklin decided to take an early retirement in 1748 at age forty-two.**

A. Though often cited as the prototype of the American capitalist, Franklin lacked the true spirit of capitalism.

1. He never truly valued money as an end in itself.

2. He thought many things were more interesting than simply making money.

B. As his business grew, he had engaged a partner, David Hall, who proved efficient and trustworthy.

1. Franklin turned the operation of the business over to Hall in 1748.

2. While he retained half of the profits, he was able to pursue what he felt were more worthy goals.

C. He explained: "I am settling my old accounts and hope soon to be quite a master of my own time, and no longer, as the song has it, at every one's call but my own. . . . I am in a fair way of having no other tasks than such as I shall like to give myself, and of enjoying what I look upon as a great happiness, leisure to read, study, make experiments, and converse at large with such ingenious and worthy men are pleased to honour me with their friendship or acquaintance, on such points as might produce something for the common benefit of mankind, uninterrupted by the little cares and fatigues of business."

II. **Enlightenment science contributed to the general development of colonial activity.**

A. In Franklin's day, philosophy still included science.

1. His American Philosophical Society was chiefly concerned with scientific research.

2. Philosophers attempted to find practical answers to life experiences rather than simply general meanings for human existence.

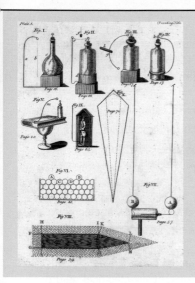

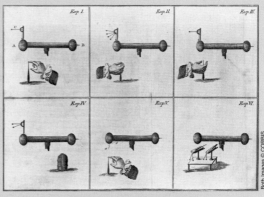

Experiments in Electricity
Benjamin Franklin's electrical apparatus and lightning rods as depicted in his book *Experiments and Observations on Electricity*.

B. Science was still the domain of amateurs, typically men like Franklin, with a measure of wealth and the leisure to indulge their curiosity about the world.

C. The key to modern science was its willingness to question assumptions.

    1. Knowledge was treated as tentative, able to be disproved through careful observation.

    2. Scientists devised experiments to reveal the validity or invalidity of premises and hypotheses.

D. The 18th century was the era of the Enlightenment, where the scientific method separated inquiry from religion.

    1. Religion preferenced revelation and faith.

    2. Science took nothing on faith, but sought to reason and test as the key to knowledge.

III. **Franklin was well equipped to tackle the questions of electricity.**

A. He was the ideal Enlightenment scientist (or philosopher).

    1. He was skeptical of everything.

    2. He was a keen observer.

    3. He could frame questions that went to the heart of puzzling phenomena.

B. Electricity was particularly susceptible to his talents.

    1. Electrical phenomena had been known for millennia, but only recently had investigators begun examining them systematically.

    2. It remained as much vaudeville (had that genre existed then) as science, with "electricians" touring the colonies giving demonstrations.

    3. Franklin attended such a demonstration and decided to put his talents to use in that area.

    4. The field was immature, meaning that a novice could get up to speed in fairly short order.

5. The apparatus required was not inordinately expensive, meaning that he could fund his research from his own pocket.

IV. **Through reason and scientific inquiry, Franklin came up with remarkable discoveries about electricity.**

A. Franklin's contributions to the field fell into two categories.

1. He provided a vocabulary summarizing current knowledge.

2. With static electricity generators, batteries, and capacitors, he reproduced experiments he had read about, as well as devising experiments of his own.

   i. He originated the terms "positive" and "negative" to unify theories that heretofore had hypothesized two different kinds of electricity.

   ii. In the process he electrocuted chickens for dinner and almost electrocuted himself.

   iii. More spectacularly, he unified observations in the laboratory with those in the real world, confirming the essentially electrical nature of lightning.

B. In 1750 Franklin proposed his famous experiment to the British Royal Society.

1. It was first conducted successfully in France.

2. Before Franklin got word of the success, he performed a variant himself, employing a kite.

C. The lightning experiment, in addition to Franklin's other contributions, won him international acclaim.

1. The Royal Society awarded Franklin its Copley Medal.

2. The French crown declared that Franklin deserved the "esteem of our nation."

3. The rest of continental Europe sung his praises.

Benjamin Franklin Performing Experiment

The first lightning-conductors placed on the house of Benjamin West by Franklin dramatically revealed their benefits when struck by lightning.

© Bettmann/CORBIS

Summary: Though he took the worldwide plaudits he gained from his electrical experiments with a grain of salt, at age forty-seven, the poor boy from Boston couldn't help taking pride in knowing he was one of the most famous men on Earth. His fame in the area of science would make Franklin a memorable historic figure, regardless of whether he had ever become involved with the American Revolution.

The "Kite Experiment"

— from *The Pennsylvania Gazette*, October 19, 1752

As frequent Mention is made in the News Papers from Europe, of the Success of the Philadelphia Experiment for drawing the Electric Fire from Clouds by Means of pointed Rods of Iron erected on high Buildings, &c. it may be agreeable to the Curious to be inform'd, that the same Experiment has succeeded in Philadelphia, tho' made in a different and more easy Manner, which any one may try, as follows.

Make a small Cross of two light Strips of Cedar, the Arms so long as to reach to the four Corners of a large thin Silk Handkerchief when extended; tie the Corners of the Handkerchief to the Extremities of the Cross, so you have the Body of a Kite; which being properly accommodated with a Tail, Loop and String, will rise in the Air, like those made of Paper; but this being of Silk is fitter to bear the Wet and Wind of a Thunder Gust without tearing. To the Top of the upright Stick of the Cross is to be fixed a very sharp pointed Wire, rising a Foot or more above the Wood. To the End of the Twine, next the Hand, is to be tied a silk Ribbon, and where the Twine and the silk join, a Key may be fastened. This Kite is to be raised when a Thunder Gust appears to be coming on, and the Person who holds the String must stand within a Door, or Window, or under some Cover, so that the Silk Ribbon may not be wet; and Care must be taken that the Twine does not touch the Frame of the Door or Window.

As soon as any of the Thunder Clouds come over the Kite, the pointed Wire will draw the Electric Fire from them, and the Kite, with all the Twine, will be electrified, and the loose Filaments of the Twine will stand out every Way, and be attracted by an approaching Finger. And when the Rain has wet the Kite and Twine, so that it can conduct the Electric Fire freely, you will find it stream out plentifully from the Key on the Approach of your Knuckle. At this Key the Phial may be charg'd; and from Electric Fire thus obtain'd, Spirits may be kindled, and all the other Electric Experiments be perform'd, which are usually done by the Help of a rubbed Glass Globe or Tube; and thereby the Sameness of the Electric Matter with that of Lightning compleatly demonstrated.

AMERICAN PHILOSOPHICAL SOCIETY

The American Philosophical Society Building

The American Philosophical Society, the oldest learned society in the United States, was formed by Benjamin Franklin in 1743.

The American Philosophical Society is an international organization that promotes excellence and useful knowledge in the sciences and humanities through scholarly research, professional meetings, publications, library resources, and community service.

It was founded in 1743 by Benjamin Franklin, who also offered to serve as its first secretary, in a paper entitled "A Proposal for Promoting Useful Knowledge Among the British Plantations in America." Membership would be extended to scientists and thinkers throughout the colonies, who would receive abstracts four times a year of what their fellow APS members were doing.

In the 18th-century natural philosophy—the study of nature—comprised the kinds of investigations now considered scientific and technological. Members of the American Philosophical Society encouraged America's economic independence by improving agriculture, manufacturing, and transportation.

Among the subjects for investigation, according to the proposal, were "newly discovered plants, herbs, trees, roots, their virtues, uses, etc. . . . improvements of vegetable juices such as ciders, wines, etc.; new methods of curing diseases . . . improvements in any branch of mathematics . . . new arts, trades, and manufactures . . . surveys, maps, and charts . . . methods for improving the breeds of animals . . . and all philosophical experiments that let light into the nature of things."

Greatly contributing to the Society's international fame was its participation in astronomical observations of the 1760s. With one of his telescopes, erected on a platform behind the State House (now Independence Hall), David Rittenhouse plotted the transit of Venus, thus attracting the recognition of the scholarly world.

The Society's library houses manuscripts and printed collections documenting the history of science, the library's primary focus; other areas covered include medicine, technology, Native North American linguistics, anthropology, and early American culture.

The library also has in its collection one of the original copies of the Declaration of Independence; a large collection of Benjamin Franklin's letters, books, and experimental equipment; the Charter of Privileges issued by William Penn, founder of the former colony of Pennsylvania; and the original Lewis and Clark journals.

Francis Hopkinson, a signer of the Declaration of Independence, and Samuel Vaughan, an immigrant, led the revival of the Society after the Revolution.

In 1780 Pennsylvania had granted it a charter guaranteeing that the APS might correspond with learned individuals and institutions "of any nation or country" on its legitimate business at all times "whether in peace or war."

The state also deeded to the Society a portion of present-day Independence Square, on which it erected Philosophical Hall in 1785-1789.

In later years, President Thomas Jefferson, also the Society's third president, involved the Society in the Lewis and Clark Expedition (1804-1806), which he commissioned.

FOR GREATER UNDERSTANDING

Consider

1. Was Franklin's early retirement consistent with his own personal moral code about the importance of hard work to a successful life?

2. Does the fact that Franklin never wrote up his results of the kite experiment call into doubt whether he actually ever performed the experiment?

3. What are some of the key similarities and differences between science in Franklin's day and science today?

Suggested Reading

Tucker, Tom. Bolt of Fate. New York: Public Affairs, 2003.

Fortune, Brandon B. and Deborah J. Warner. Franklin & His Friends: Portraying the Man of Science in Eighteenth-Century America. Philadelphia: University of Pennsylvania Press, 1999.

Other Books of Interest

Goodman, Nathan G., ed. The Ingenious Dr. Franklin: Selected Scientific Letters of Benjamin Franklin. Philadelphia: University of Pennsylvania Press, 2000.

Websites to Visit

1. http://www.ushistory.org/franklin/kite/ - The Electric Franklin.

2. http://www.masshist.org/cabinet/december2002/december2002.htm - This site contains links to excerpts from a letter written by Benjamin Franklin to John Franklin describing Benjamin Franklin's attempt to "kill a Turkey by Shock." Links to both pages of the letter—as high-resolution images—are also available.

Before beginning this lecture you may want to . . .

Read H.W. Brands' The First American, Chapter 10.

Introduction:

Despite Franklin's desire to spend his retirement in the study of scientific questions, and despite the successes he achieved in his studies in the area of electricity, he would soon become distracted from his philosophical pursuits. Rather than being pulled from his scientitific studies by business, however, he was instead drawn more clearly into the public sphere of politics.

Consider this . . .

1. How had the extended series of wars between France and Great Britain helped to shape colonists' perceptions of their position in the world?

2. What events led Franklin to first consider the importance of union for the colonies in America?

I. **World politics in the mid-18th century affected America.**

A. Since the late 17th century, Britain and France had been locked in a contest for control of North America.

1. This rivalry grew out of the earlier rivalry touched off when Spain and Portugal set out from Iberia seeking new routes to the (East) Indies.

2. Tiny Portugal lost ground once its larger European neighbors got into the race.

3. Spain had been eclipsed when most of its Grand Armada sank off the coast of England in 1588.

4. While Spain still controlled most of Central and South America, north of Mexico the contest was between Britain and France.

B. France and Britain fought four wars between the 1690s and the 1760s.

1. In each case the British North American colonies felt the weight of French attacks, especially the attacks of Indians allied to France.

2. During most of Franklin's adult life, the question of colonial defense was the most pressing issue of provincial politics.

II. **Franklin's entrance into politics was not wholly through his own choice.**

A. Franklin's talents and inclinations inevitably led people to see his political potential.

B. Franklin hesitated to enter politics, feeling he had the wrong temperament.

C. He was drafted to run for the Philadelphia town council and later was elected to the provincial assembly.

1. He got into disputes over whether the Penn family (the "proprietors") were paying their fair share of colonial expenses, especially relating to defense.

2. Franklin spearheaded committees that criticized the Penns and their handpicked agents, the provincial governors.

D. The failure of colonial defense prompted Franklin to propose a provincial militia.

1. It provided the people of Pennsylvania with a sense of security.

2. It led the Penns to fear a provincial revolution.

3. Franklin was deemed the ringleader and consequently most dangerous.

E. As part of his defense work, Franklin was appointed to negotiate with various Indian tribes.

1. Franklin recognized that the Indians had been regularly cheated out of their land.

2. He urged that the province and the imperial government live up to their commitments.

3. He also recommended in the strongest terms that Indian traders be prevented from supplying the Indians with liquor, which corrupted them and made them prey to those who would defraud them.

III. **Franklin recognized the need for union to defend the North American colonies.**

A. Lack of unity on the part of the colonies allowed the French and the Indians to play one colony against another, diminishing the security of all.

B. The problem was exacerbated by cost-cutting in London.

1. British taxpayers resented having to defend the distant frontier against Indians who were simply reacting to the provocation of speculators, traders, and other colonists.

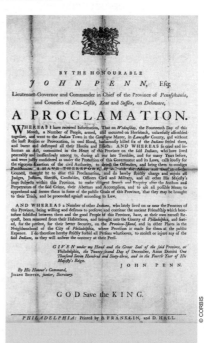

© CORBIS

Franklin Lobbies

Proclamation issued by Pennsylvania Lt. Governor John Penn after a massacre of Indians by colonists in Lancaster County.

Franklin urged the Penns to take action over incidents such as this to help prevent Native Americans from retaliation by allying with the French (or other more warlike tribes) and create further bloodshed on the western frontier.

Franklin printed this and other proclamations.

2. As a result, there were never enough soldiers to protect the frontier—which in those days was often not more than a day or two's ride from the centers of population.

C. Upon the outbreak of the last of the four wars called the French and Indian War in America, Franklin proposed a colonial union.

1. At a congress held in Albany in 1754, he collaborated with Thomas Hutchinson in promoting a plan of union.

2. Franklin's draft called for a "grand council" of delegates from each colony (chosen according to population, as later in the U.S. House of Representatives).

3. The executive would be a "president general," who would conduct diplomacy and be commander-in-chief during war.

4. The separate colonies would retain their individual governments (as would the states under the Constitution of 1787).

5. The Albany Congress approved the plan.

   i. Franklin helped publicize the union with a famous cartoon (the first political cartoon in American history) showing a snake cut into several pieces, labeled for the separate colonies.

   ii. The cartoon's caption was "Join, or Die."

D. The Congress referred the plan to the colonies and to the British Parliament. "How they will relish it, or how it will be looked on in England," Franklin told a friend, "I know not."

E. In fact, nothing came of Franklin's union plan—at that point.

   i. Provincial jealousies and imperial politics got in the way.

   ii. In this plan, Franklin planted a seed that would sprout again, with far greater effect, two decades later, in the events leading up to the Revolutionary War.

Summary: Though reluctantly drafted into political life, Franklin undertook his new duties with the same energy and clear thinking he had previously shown in business and scientific enquiry. His recommendations for a union to protect the colonies from frontier threats were a clear precursor to the type of unity that would be necessary in the coming decades as America moved toward revolution.

Illustration of Benjamin Franklin's "Join, or Die" snake.

THE FRENCH AND INDIAN WAR

The last of the colonial conflicts that France and Great Britain fought in North America shaped the destiny of America. It cost France its North American empire and the strains in the relationship between Britain and its colonies led to the American Revolution.

Beginning in 1689, Britain fought a series of wars with France, known in America as King William's War (1689-1697), Queen Anne's War (1702-1713), and finally King George's War (1744-1748).

In 1745 New England militiamen captured the French naval fortress of Louisbourg on Cape Breton Island (near the mouth of the St. Lawrence River), but the Treaty of Aix-la-Chapelle (1748) returned the fortress to France—not without considerable resentment on the part of the Americans who had fought so hard to take it.

The final conflict in America was the French and Indian War. It began in the struggle for control of the Ohio Valley, where the powerful Iroquois Confederacy dominated a middle ground between the French and British colonies in North America.The Iroquois maintained their power against that of both the British and the French until the 1740s when the Ohio Company, an association of land speculators based in Virginia, encouraged the movement of traders and settlers into the region. These developments convinced the French to reinforce their existing forts south of Lake Erie and expel the British from the forks of the Ohio. At that strategic site, they built a new military post, Fort Duquesne, and established firm title to the region.

In answer, a party of Virginians under the command of George Washington defeated a small French force east of the Ohio River and built a log stockade that became known as Fort Necessity.

The French laid siege to this small fort (a log stockade), forcing Washington and his troops to surrender on July 4, 1754. They sent Washington and his troops back to Virginia. The French and Indian War had begun.

The British urged the colonial governors to seek an alliance with the Iroquois Confederacy, often referred to as the Six Nations.

In June 1754 delegates from seven colonies met with 150 Iroquois leaders in Albany, New York. Some members of the Iroquois Confederacy already in alliances with the British colonies complained of poor treatment and said the British governor of Virginia attempted to seize their lands. But large presents of supplies and arms convinced the Iroquois to renew their alliances with the British colonies.

Reconstructed Fort Necessity

Fort Necessity, the site of George Washington's surrender of his Virginia Provincial troops to the French on July 4, 1754, was reconstructed at the Fort Necessity National Battlefield in Farmington, Pennsylvania.

Braddock's Defeat

Mortally wounded, General Edward Braddock (1695-1755) is shown being carried off the battlefield at his defeat after an ambush by French forces and their Indian allies.

Delegates moved on to other measures such as the plan of union developed by Benjamin Franklin. The "Albany Plan," as it came to be known, proposed a single institution to govern all of the British colonies in America.

Under the plan, each colony would send delegates to an American continental assembly, presided over by a British governor-general. This council would assume responsibility for the western affairs of the colonies, including trade, Native American policy, and defense.

The Albany Plan was never implemented because the British government feared the consequences of convening a great American assembly, and individual colonial assemblies refused to support the proposal because they wanted to preserve their autonomy.

During the next five years, the government sent thousands of regular troops under a succession of British commanders. In addition, Parliament financed the enlistment and supply of more than 20,000 American troops from 1758 to 1760.

During the early part of the war, the French ambushed and defeated forces led by British General Edward Braddock before they could attack Fort Duquesne. Braddock was killed and more than 900 of his men were killed or wounded. British and colonial forces offset these losses by the capture of Nova Scotia, from which they deported over 6,000 of the French inhabitants, known as Acadians.

In mid-1756 a French force captured the British fort at Oswego in northern New York. In 1757 they defeated British regulars and New England militia at Fort William Henry, within striking distance of the important fur-trading town of Albany, New York.

But the small French Canadian population was not large enough to provide food and soldiers for a lengthy campaign, and so the advantage was lost. The British, however, could call upon a population more than ten times as large to provide troops and supplies.

Strong support by the British government began after William Pitt became secretary of state in June 1757. The next year, a force of 16,000 British and colonial troops advanced from Albany toward Montréal, but stalled in the face of French opposition at Fort Ticonderoga in northeastern New York.

However, British and colonial troops under General Jeffrey Amherst took the fortress of Louisbourg on Cape Breton Island near the mouth of the St. Lawrence River. Additional British victories came at Fort Frontenac, on Lake Ontario, and at Fort Duquesne.

Bolstered by these successes, William Pitt ordered a new British offensive for 1759. The British captured Fort Niagara at the junction of lakes Erie and Ontario and forced the French to abandon the strategic Fort Ticonderoga.

Late in 1759 British troops led by James Wolfe defeated a French army commanded by Louis Joseph Marquis de Montcalm de Saint-Véran on the Plains of

Abraham, just outside Québec. The capture of the fortified city of Québec was the climax of the "year of victories" for Great Britain. Only Montréal remained in French hands, and it surrendered to British forces in September 1760.

When warfare ended in 1763, William Pitt had left office, but Britain controlled over half the North American continent, including French Canada, all French territorial claims east of the Mississippi River, and Spanish Florida.

All that was left to France was a handful of sugar plantations in the West Indies and two rocky islands off the coast of Newfoundland.

Before the war, Britain gave its colonies largely free rein. As long as few serious conflicts of interest arose between Britain and its American possessions, the British government permitted colonial assemblies to oversee enforcement of instructions of the royal governors or to pass new legislation suited to their own needs.

As a result, the colonists developed a political and economic system that was virtually independent. They were loyal, although somewhat uncooperative, subjects of the crown.

The British were concerned about the colonists' lack of cooperation during the French and Indian War. They resented the fact that the prosperous colonists were unwilling to undertake their own defense.

Even generous subsidies voted by Parliament at William Pitt's urging did not cause the colonists to respond as the British expected.

Colonial assemblies refused to send their militiamen on expeditions to Canada, claiming that their militias were needed at home. They also demanded greater authority over finances and military appointments in return for their approval of war-related measures.

The royal governors, under strict orders from the British ministry to support the war effort in America, often gave in to these demands without resistance.

In addition, many Americans continued to trade illegally with France. Smuggling was highly profitable and prolonged the war by sustaining the French sugar plantations in the West Indies and providing the French armies with food and supplies.

This led to British demands for more centralized control. The British government also faced pressing financial problems. Britain began fighting in 1754 with a national debt of approximately 75 million pounds, but the war effort caused the debt to soar to 133 million pounds by 1763.

Americans had benefited substantially from these military expenditures. They had received a million pounds in direct subsidies and millions more in contracts for food, supplies, and transport for the British military forces in America.

After these huge expenses, Britain was reluctant to offer additional subsidies for the peacetime defense of the colonies. Money was needed to maintain British troops in Canada, Florida, and a chain of western frontier posts. Taxing the colonies seemed the natural answer.

For the colonists, the French and Indian War increased their concern over the permanent presence of a British army. They believed that a standing army threatened liberty and representative government.

These fears intensified as the British demanded imperial reform, imposed direct taxes, and stationed army units in the colonial port cities. This led the colonists to active rebellion and, ultimately, independence.

FOR GREATER UNDERSTANDING

Consider

1. What makes a person an effective leader?

2. How were Franklin's early efforts to create a secure union among the colonies similar to the activities he undertook in improving the city of Philadelphia as a young businessman?

Suggested Reading

Anderson, Fred. Crucible of War: The Seven Years' War and the Fate of Empire in British North America, 1754-1766. New York: Knopf, 2000.

Brumwell, Stephen. Redcoats: The British Soldier and War in the Americas. Cambridge (UK): Cambridge University Press, 2001.

Waddell, Louis M., Bruce D. Bomberger and the Pennsylvania Historical and Museum Commission. The French and Indian War in Pennsylvania, 1753-1763: Fortification and Struggle During the War for Empire. Harrisburg, PA: Pennsylvania Historical and Museum Commission, 1997.

Other Books of Interest

Rogers, Robert, Timothy J. Todish and Gary S. Zaboly. The Annotated and Illustrated Journals of Major Robert Rogers. Fleischmanns, NY: Purple Mountain Press, Ltd., 2001.

Skaarup, Harold A. and Frederick C. Burnett. Ticonderoga Soldier Elijah Estabrooks Journal, 1758-1760: A Massachusetts Provincial Soldier in the French and Indian War. Lincoln, NE: iUniverse.com, 2001.

Websites to Visit

1. http://odur.let.rug.nl/~usa/H/1994/ch2_p7.htm - This site gives a brief but factual outline of the French and Indian War.

2. http://earlyamerica.com/review/spring97/newspapers.html - A comprehensive account of the French and Indian War on American soil as reported in newspapers of the day.

Before beginning this lecture you may want to . . .

Read H.W. Brands' The First American, Chapters 11-16.

Introduction:

By the time he was fifty years old, Franklin's social and political involvement had moved from concerns about improving Philadelphia to efforts for securing Pennsylvania to, finally, an interest in what he could do to improve life in all of the British American colonies. While he still considered himself a loyal subject of Great Britain, like many other people in the colonies at this time, he was beginning to develop an identity that was distinctly American. The imperial problems that would eventually lead to the American Revolution continued to move Franklin toward a position favoring colonial independence during the period following the French and Indian Wars.

Consider this . . .

1. What peacetime actions by the British government drew the sharpest distinctions between the interests of British citizens in the old world and concerns of those in the new world?

2. What events led Franklin to become a colonial agent to Great Britain?

I. **Britain won the French and Indian Wars, but eventually lost the peace that followed.**

   A. In 1763 Britain and her American colonies (and their Indian allies) won the war against France and her Indian allies.

   1. The Americans celebrated, expecting that the expulsion of France from North America would at last leave their frontiers in peace.

   2. Colonists hoped to see the way opened to additional settlement in the Ohio Valley and elsewhere beyond the Appalachian mountains.

   B. The British government saw things differently.

   1. The war had been very expensive, and the first order of business in London was putting imperial affairs on a sound footing.

   2. This required cutting costs and increasing revenues.

   C. To cut costs, Britain determined to pull troops back from the frontier.

   1. This required—or seemed to require—reducing the occasion for clashes between colonists and Indians.

   2. London drew a line at the crest of the Appalachians, beyond which the colonists were not allowed to settle.

   3. This Proclamation of 1763 seemed to the colonists a denial of all that they had fought for.

D. To increase revenues, Britain enacted new taxes.

   1. The Sugar Act of 1764 reduced the rate on molasses imported into the American colonies.

      i. It promised to increase the revenues, as now it would be cheaper to pay the duty than to smuggle.

      ii. The Act also called for stiffer enforcement.

   2. The more controversial Stamp Act of 1765 taxed licenses, deeds, newspapers, almanacs, playing cards, dice, and other items used by ordinary people in everyday life.

      i. This tax angered ordinary citizens.

      ii. It angered newspaper editors and lawyers.

      iii. The new tax was more obvious than simply increasing an old tax.

II. **Franklin observed the imperial reorganization with concern but not alarm.**

   A. A Pennsylvania political controversy led to Franklin's service as a colonial agent.

      1. In January 1757, almost at the moment he turned fifty-one, Franklin's colleagues in the Pennsylvania Assembly appointed him their agent to the British Parliament.

      2. His initial task was to argue for reform of the charter under which the Penn family governed (or misgoverned, in the colonists' eyes) Pennsylvania.

      3. Ironically, the Assembly wanted Franklin to push for an increase of royal control.

   B. En route to London, Franklin penned one of his two most famous works.

      1. It was an attempt to retire "Poor Richard" with a kind of "greatest hits" collection.

      2. It became commonly reprinted under the title *The Way to Wealth*.

      3. This short pamphlet was widely successful.

      4. This gave Franklin a reputation as a money-grubbing grind.

   C. Franklin's initial reception in England was difficult.

      1. The Penns threw hurdles in his path.

      2. The British government was unimpressed by his scientific fame.

   D. On the whole he found London most congenial.

      1. He formed close friendships with fellow scientists and others who had come to admire him from a distance.

      2. He might well have relocated to London permanently—his friends urged him to do so—had Debbie not refused to join him.

© Bettmann/CORBIS

THE STAMP ACT

The Stamp Act was introduced by British prime minister George Grenville and passed by the British Parliament on March 22, 1765, as a means of raising revenue in the American colonies.

The Stamp Act required all legal documents, licenses, commercial contracts, newspapers, pamphlets, and playing cards to carry a tax stamp. It extended to the colonies the system of stamp duties then employed in Great Britain.

The money collected by the Stamp Act was to be used to help pay the costs of defending and protecting the American frontier near the Appalachian Mountains (10,000 troops were to be stationed on the American frontier for this purpose).

Passed without debate, it aroused widespread opposition among the colonists, who argued that because they were not represented in Parliament, they could not legally be taxed without their consent.

The actual cost of the Stamp Act was relatively small. What made the law so offensive to the colonists was not so much its immediate cost but the standard it seemed to set. In the past, taxes and duties on colonial trade had always been viewed as measures to regulate commerce, not to raise money.

The Stamp Act, however, was viewed as a direct attempt by England to raise money in the colonies without the approval of the colonial legislatures. If this new tax were allowed to pass without resistance, the colonists reasoned, the door would be open for far more troublesome taxation in the future.

A Stamp Act Congress of delegates from nine of the American colonies convened in October 1765 at New York City to protest against the Stamp Act. It included representatives of Massachusetts, New York, New Jersey, Rhode Island, Pennsylvania, Delaware, Connecticut, Maryland, and South Carolina.

The delegates expressed the opposition of the colonists to the oppressive Stamp Act in three documents: a Declaration of Rights and Grievances, an address to the king, and a group of petitions to both houses of the British Parliament.

Although the congress recognized the authority of Parliament, its petitions were refused for formal consideration by the House of Commons as coming from an unauthorized body.

The Stamp Act was repealed in 1766, largely as a result of pressure from British business interests.

The principles of independence enunciated by the congress, such as the right of trial by jury and particularly the ringing denunciation of "taxation without representation," were later adopted by the leaders of the American Revolution and were incorporated into such revolutionary instruments as the Declaration of Independence.

III. **The emerging political crisis over Britain's imperial control of the colonies altered Franklin's role as a colonial agent.**

   A. Amid the emerging struggle between the colonies and Parliament, Franklin's original reason for going to London was forgotten.

      1. Hardliners in Parliament wanted the colonies to pay still more.

      2. Radicals in America refused to pay anything.

      3. Franklin's temperament suited him to act as a mediator.

         i. He lobbied against the Sugar Act, but wasn't surprised that it passed over his opposition.

         ii. He told the Parliament that it was making a mistake with the Stamp Act, which trampled on the colonists' rights as Englishmen to have a say in their own taxation. Again his dissent was ignored.

         iii. He hoped to have the measure repealed, but until it was, he thought to make what use he could of it. "We might as well have hindered the sun's setting. That we could not do. But since 'tis down, my friend, and it may be long before it rises again, let us make as good a night of it as we can."

         iv. He nominated a friend to be a stamp commissioner, and was pleased when he got the job.

   B. Franklin was shocked when he discovered the depth of American opposition.

      1. Riots broke out up and down the Atlantic seaboard.

      2. Stamp commissioners were browbeaten and forced to resign.

      3. Thomas Hutchinson's house was demolished by rioters in Boston.

   C. Franklin was branded a collaborator by some of the radicals.

      1. An angry mob in Philadelphia vowed to level his house.

         i. Debbie rallied friends to her and his defense, and they managed to avoid the wrath of the rioters.

         ii. "I honour much the spirit and courage you showed," he wrote her. "The woman deserves a good house that is determined to defend it."

      2. Beneath his congratulations to Debbie, he knew he had made a grave political misstep.

      3. The only way to rectify his error was to redouble his efforts to repeal the act that started all the trouble.

Summary: Sent to London to deal with issues of concern only to Pennsylvanians, Franklin soon found himself in the midst of a much larger, more impassioned dispute having to do with all the colonies. Though initially slow to gauge the depth of feeling on each side of the taxation issue, Franklin understood the need to increase his diplomatic efforts when he realized the dangerous passion that the subject was inspiring.

LECTURE EIGHT

TARRING AND FEATHERING

Tarring and feathering dates back to the days of the Crusades and King Richard the Lionhearted. The earliest mention of the punishment occurs in the orders of Richard I of England, issued to his navy on starting for the Holy Land in 1191.

"Concerning the lawes and ordinances appointed by King Richard for his navie the forme thereof was this . . . item, a thiefe or felon that hath stolen, being lawfully convicted, shal have his head shorne, and boyling pitch poured upon his head, and feathers or downe strawed upon the same whereby he may be knowen, and so at the first landing-place they shall come to, there to be cast up." (Translation of the original statute in *Hakluy's Voyages, ii. 21*)

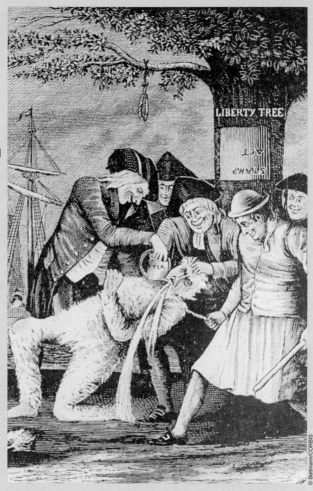

Bostonians tar and feather a British tax collector.

A later instance of this penalty being inflicted is given in *Notes and Queries* (series 4, vol. v.), which quotes one James Howell writing from Madrid, in 1623, of the "boisterous Bishop of Halverstadt," who, "having taken a place where there were two monasteries of nuns and friars, he caused divers feather beds to be ripped, and all the feathers thrown into a great hall, whither the nuns and friars were thrust naked with their bodies oiled and pitched and to tumble among these feathers, which makes them here (Madrid) presage him an ill-death."

In 1696 a London bailiff, who attempted to serve process on a debtor who had taken refuge within the precincts of the Savoy, was tarred and feathered and taken in a wheelbarrow to the Strand, where he was tied to the maypole that stood by what is now Somerset House.

In the American colonies, the Stamp Act of 1765 aroused a lot of angry opposition before the Revolution. What outraged colonists was not so much the tax as the fact that it was being imposed from England. Reaction to the Stamp Act in the colonies was swift and, on occasion, riotous.

Seeking to pressure and intimidate the officials tasked to implement this law, those who opposed the measure threatened the officials with being tarred and feathered.

In Massachusetts, rioters ransacked the home of the newly appointed stamp commissioner, Andrew Oliver. He resigned the position the next day.

Threatening or attacking the Crown-appointed office-holders became a popular tactic against the act throughout the colonies. By November 1, 1765, the day the Stamp Act was to officially take effect, there was not a single stamp commissioner left in the colonies to collect the tax.

Though no stamp commissioner was actually tarred and feathered, this medieval brutality was a popular form of 18th-century mob violence in Great Britain, particularly against tax collectors.

It was also a typical punishment used to enforce justice on the early American frontier. Both tar used in construction and feathers from food sources (e.g., chickens) were plentiful in the middle United States, where the practice primarily flourished.

The idea was to hurt and humiliate a person enough so they would leave town and cause no more mischief. Hot tar was either poured or painted on to a criminal while he (rarely she) was immobilized.

Then the person either had feathers thrown on him from buckets or barrels or else he was thrown into a pile of them and rolled around. Then the victim was taken to the edge of town and set free in the hopes he would not return. The feathers would stick to the tar for days, making the person's sentence clear to the public.

While this practice was extremely cruel it was usually an effective manner of exile. It was eventually abandoned because it did nothing to rehabilitate its victims of the criminal behavior for which they were sentenced.

Tar and feathering began to appear in New England seaports in the 1760s and was most often used by patriot mobs against loyalists. Tar was readily available in shipyards and feathers came from any handy pillow.

Though the cruelty invariably stopped short of murder, the tar needed to be burning hot for application.

The image of the tarred-and-feathered outlaw is so vivid that the expression remains a metaphor for a humiliating public castigation, many years after the practice disappeared.

FOR GREATER UNDERSTANDING

Consider

1. How might the history of the American Revolution been different if Debbie had come to London to live with Franklin?

2. Did Franklin's personality as an apostle of reason limit his effectiveness among advocates who preferred passion?

Suggested Reading

Franklin, Benjamin. The Way to Wealth. Bedford, MA: Applewood Books, 1986.

Morgan, Edmund S. and Helen M. Morgan. The Stamp Act Crisis. Chapel Hill: University of North Carolina Press, 1995.

Other Books of Interest

Coldham, Peter W. American Migrations, 1765-1799: The Lives, Times and Families of Colonial Americans Who Remained Loyal to the British Crown Before, During and After the Revolutionary War. Baltimore: Genealogical Publishing Co., Inc., 2000.

Websites to Visit

1. http://www.pbs.org/ktca/liberty/chronicle/stampactriots-tar.html - A one-page description on the practice of tar and feathering as a result of the Stamp Act.

2. http://www.historycarper.com/resources/docs/sugaract.htm - The Sugar Act of 1764 appears in its entirety.

Before beginning this lecture you may want to . . .

Read H.W. Brands' The First American, Prologue and Chapters 17-21.

Introduction

As he reached his later years, Franklin—like the American colonies—was forced to reconsider the nature of his identity. A diplomat in Britain during the time when tensions were greatest, Franklin tried unsuccessfully to serve as a mediator between the two sides, before finally realizing that his real identity—and his true loyalties—must lie with America.

Consider this . . .

1. Why did Franklin work so hard to mend the growing rift between the government of Great Britain and the American colonies?

2. In what ways did Franklin try to mediate between the two sides in the growing disputes between Britain and her colonies in America? How effective were these attempts?

I. **The stakes of empire were high.**

  A. No one, and especially not Franklin, knew precisely what was at stake in the unrest that had been fomented by the Stamp Act.

    1. Tax riots were fairly common in Britain.

    2. It was easy to conclude in Britain that life would go on.

    3. Americans felt that their rights as British citizens were under threat.

    4. Lack of representation made things more serious from the colonists' standpoint.

  B. Franklin was a great enthusiast of the British empire, and he felt the political rift could still be mended.

    1. He may have been the most famous British subject of his day.

    2. His son William was the colonial governor of New Jersey.

    3. His vision was of America growing within the empire.

    4. His work on population growth indicated that the colonies would soon be the larger, stronger part of the British empire.

    5. Franklin saw the future as a union of equals within the British empire.

  C. This vision prompted him to remain a great imperialist and try to do whatever he could to keep the empire from falling apart.

II. **The rift between Britain and the American colonies was widening.**

  A. Franklin's view was hardly the consensus, certainly not in America.

1. The radicals increasingly held the upper hand, compelling those who disagreed to keep silent.
2. The Stamp Act riots were less against the British than against disagreeing Americans—like Franklin's friend John Hughes, the stamp commissioner.
3. Besides the rioting, the chief weapon of the resisters was the boycott.

    i. It was designed to hit Britain where it hurt, in the ledger book.

    ii. Boycotts weren't self-enforcing; again, dissenters were intimidated.

B. Radical tactics worked.
1. In 1766, Parliament repealed the Stamp Act.
2. But it also passed the Declaratory Act, affirming the right of Parliament to tax the colonies.

C. In 1767 Parliament approved a new set of taxes, called the Townshend duties, after Charles Townshend.
1. Americans paid less in taxes than other British citizens.
2. British perception was that their debt was a result of defending the colonies.

III. **Franklin saw his position as that of a conciliator.**

A. He continued to seek a middle ground.
1. Sometimes he wrote for the London papers, often anonymously.
2. He testified before Parliament, downplaying the role of the radicals in America and avowing the loyalty of the colonies to Britain.

B. He drew a distinction between internal and external taxes, saying only the external taxes were widely resented.
1. Internal taxes were levied and had to be paid within the American colonies.
2. External taxes on imports could be avoided.

C. This proved to be a tactical error when Townshend devised his list of external taxes.

Frederick Lord North

Lord North served as British Prime Minister from 1770 to 1782. It was under his ministry, and with his influence, that Alexander Wedderburn achieved status despite their notable differences. North's prosecution of the American War for Independence became a serious point of contention with hard-line ministers. Both he and King George III were later blamed for losing the American colonies.

IV. Colonial resistance increased with the levying of new taxes.

A. Franklin was embarrassed when the new taxes were resisted almost as vehemently as the Stamp Act taxes.

    1. Clearly, Americans resented all taxes.

    2. Franklin was seen as out of touch with colonial feeling.

    3. That feeling was ostensibly "no taxation without representation."

B. Hard-liners in Britain were intent on showing the Americans who was boss.

    1. They offered representation for the colonies.

    2. Americans refused representation, because what they really wanted was no taxes.

    3. Franklin feared real trouble. "The friends of both countries wish a reconciliation; the enemies of either endeavour to widen the breach. God knows how it will end."

C. Things escalated in 1770 with the "Boston Massacre."

    1. Five Bostonians were killed.

    2. Franklin decried the violence and tried to calm things, but to little avail.

D. Events escalated further with the "Boston Tea Party" of 1773.

V. Escalating events led to a fateful decision by Franklin.

A. Relaxation techniques such as cold air baths brought Franklin only minor relief.

B. Attempting to find a way out of the impasse, Franklin tried something daring—and perhaps unethical.

    1. He leaked letters from Thomas Hutchinson and Peter Oliver in Massachusetts to the British government, arguing that the English liberties of the colonists would have to be curtailed.

    2. Franklin's aim was to defuse the radical argument that the entire government was against the Americans.

    3. He felt the letters would put the blame on these few bad apples, who might be replaced.

A Privy Council

A group of animals, representing the King and his ministers, sit around a table in various stages of boredom and excitement during the American Revolution.

C. Franklin was either naive or simply wrong.

1. The letters were published—against his recommendation.
2. They inflamed the radicals in America.
3. They also inflamed British opinion against the unidentified leaker.

D. When he identified himself as the leaker, Franklin was invited to a session of the Privy Council, held in the Cockpit.

1. The session, in January 1774, just after Franklin's 68th birthday, was a two-hour diatribe against Franklin by Alexander Wedderburn, the solicitor general.
2. The attack was so slanderous that no newspaper would print it.
3. Franklin refused to dignify the slanders with a response.

E. The Privy Council session appeared to make up Franklin's mind.

1. He walked into the session an Englishman.
2. He walked out realizing that first and foremost he was an American.

Summary: Though he tried his best to act as a conciliatory voice in the growing dispute between Great Britain and the colonies over taxation, Franklin's time in London had left him out of touch with public feeling in the American colonies. As his efforts led to more and more spectacular failures, Franklin came to realize that he was no longer perceived as a British citizen, but rather as an American colonist, an identity he at last decided to embrace.

Text of Franklin's letter to The London Chronicle *admitting his role in releasing letters from several authors, but most importantly those of the Massachusetts-Bay Colony's Governor and Lt. Governor (and brothers-in-law) Thomas Hutchinson and Andrew Oliver, respectively.*

"To the PRINTER of the LONDON CHRONICLE.

SIR, Finding that two Gentlemen [Thomas Whately and John Temple –ed.] have been unfortunately engaged in a Duel, about a transaction and its circumstances of which both of them are totally ignorant and innocent, I think it incumbent on me to declare (for the prevention of farther mischief, as far as such a declaration may contribute to prevent it) that I alone am the person who obtained and transmitted to Boston the letters in question. —Mr. W. could not communicate them, because they were never in his possession; and, for the same reason, they could not be taken from him by Mr. T. —They were not of the nature of 'private letters between friends.' They were written by public officers to persons in public station, on public affairs, and intended to procure public measures; they were therefore handed to other public persons who might be influenced by them to produce those measures: Their tendency was to incense the Mother Country against her Colonies, and, by the steps recommended, to widen the breach, which they effected. The chief Caution expressed with regard to Privacy was to keep their contents from the Colony Agents, who the writers apprehended might return them, or copies of them, to America. That apprehension was, it seems, well founded; for the first Agent who laid his hands on them, thought it his duty to transmit them to his Constituents.

B. FRANKLIN, Agent for the House of Representatives of the Massachusetts-Bay. Craven-street, Dec. 25, 1773."

— from *The London Chronicle,* December 25, 1773

The Boston Massacre

Less of a so-called massacre than an otherwise forgettable street brawl gotten out of control, the event was a propaganda godsend to American radicals looking for incidents to inflame their fellow citizens against the British empire.

British troops were quartered in the city to discourage demonstrations against the Townsend Acts, which imposed duties on imports to the colonies. To supplement their pay, some British troops took odd jobs during their off-duty hours, charging less than the itinerant laborers in town who had previously depended on this work.

For this and other reasons, feelings turned bitter. Citizens constantly harassed the troops.

On Monday March 5, 1770, after a weekend of minor clashes, the conflicts between Boston Garrison soldiers and colonialists came to a head. Insults exchanged between a British soldier and a local merchant ended with a butt-stroke of a musket.

This led to a small riot, and the Boston Garrison responded with a small squad of soldiers under the command of Captain Thomas Preston. The colonial mob taunted and menaced the squad, but it wasn't until Private Hugh Montgomery was struck by a thrown club that any action occurred.

When Montgomery returned to his feet he took aim into the crowd and fired. His compatriots joined him, under no command of Preston. Three colonialists were killed and two mortally wounded.

The eight soldiers and their commanding officer were tried for murder and were defended by John Adams, later president of the United States, and Josiah Quincy.

Two soldiers were declared guilty of manslaughter and, after claiming benefit of clergy, were branded on the thumb; the others, including the officer, were acquitted.

Given the fact that he was one of the

British Troops Shooting at Crowd in Boston Massacre by Paul Revere, 1770

leaders of the American Revolution, it is ironic that John Adams was also the defense attorney in the murder trial of the British soldiers who fired into a crowd during the Boston Massacre, March 5, 1770.

As a trial lawyer, however, Adams was concerned with legal defense, not propaganda. Furthermore, he had not yet made his own break with the mother country.

Adams' summary before the court effectively made the case the soldiers were provoked into the killings (they would all be acquitted of murder), but also reflected many legal principles with which Adams and the other revolutionary leaders eventually framed the government of the United States.

As he told the court, "If you are satisfied that the people, whoever they were, made that assault, with a design to kill or maim the soldiers, this was such an assault, as will justify the soldiers killing in their own defense," adding "the law does not oblige us to bear insults to the danger of our lives, to stand still with such a number of people round us, throwing such things at us, and threatening our lives, until we are disabled to defend ourselves."

After this event, the British Troops had to evacuate Boston to nearby Castle William on Castle Island. The incident was skillfully exploited by Samuel Adams (John Adams' cousin) to create anti-British sentiment in the colonies that helped bring on the Revolution.

CAPTAIN THOMAS PRESTON'S ACCOUNT OF THE INCIDENT
(March 13, 1770)

In a detailed letter to his commanding officer, Captain Thomas Preston recounted the events of the night of March 5th. *(After three paragraphs describing the general circumstances of British troops in Boston, Captain Preston began his report.)—ed.*

"On Monday night about 8 o'clock two soldiers were attacked and beat. But the party of the townspeople in order to carry matters to the utmost length, broke into two meeting houses and rang the alarm bells, which I supposed was for fire as usual, but was soon undeceived. About 9 some of the guard came to and informed me the town inhabitants were assembling to attack the troops, and that the bells were ringing as the signal for that purpose and not for fire, and the beacon intended to be fired to bring in the distant people of the country. This, as I was captain of the day, occasioned my repairing immediately to the main guard. In my way there I saw the people in great commotion, and heard them use the most cruel and horrid threats against the troops. In a few minutes after I reached the guard, about 100 people passed it and went towards the custom house where the king's money is lodged. They immediately surrounded the sentry posted there, and with clubs and other weapons threatened to execute their vengeance on him. I was soon informed by a townsman their intention was to carry off the soldier from his post and probably murder him. On which I desired him to return for further intelligence, and

he soon came back and assured me he heard the mob declare they would murder him. This I feared might be a prelude to their plundering the king's chest. I immediately sent a non-commissioned officer and 12 men to protect both the sentry and the king's money, and very soon followed myself to prevent, if possible, all disorder, fearing lest the officer and soldiers, by the insults and provocations of the rioters, should be thrown off their guard and commit some rash act.

"They soon rushed through the people, and by charging their bayonets in half-circles, kept them at a little distance. Nay, so far was I from intending the death of any person that I suffered the troops to go to the spot where the unhappy affair took place without any loading in their pieces; nor did I ever give orders for loading them. This remiss conduct in me perhaps

> *"The mob still increased and were more outrageous, striking their clubs or bludgeons one against another, and calling out, 'Come on you rascals, you bloody backs, you lobster scoundrels, fire if you dare, G-d damn you, fire and be damned, we know you dare not!'"*

merits censure; yet it is evidence, resulting from the nature of things, which is the best and surest that can be offered, that my intention was not to act offensively, but the contrary part, and that not without compulsion. The mob still increased and were more outrageous, striking their clubs or bludgeons one against another, and calling out, 'Come on you rascals, you bloody backs, you lobster scoundrels, fire if you dare, G-d damn you, fire and be damned, we know you dare not,' and much more such language was used. At this time I was between the soldiers and the mob, parleying with, and endeavouring all in my power to persuade them to retire peaceably, but to no purpose. They advanced to the points of the bayonets, struck some of them and even the muzzles of the pieces, and seemed to be endeavouring to close with the soldiers. On which some well behaved persons asked me if the guns were charged. I replied 'Yes.' They then asked me if I intended to order the men to fire. I answered 'No, by no means,' observing to them that I was advanced before the muzzles of the men's pieces, and must fall a sacrifice if they fired; that the soldiers were upon the half cock and charged bayonets, and my giving the word fire under those circumstances would prove me to be no officer.

"While I was thus speaking, one of the soldiers having received a severe blow with a stick, stepped a little on one side and instantly fired, on which turning to and asking him why he fired without orders, I was struck with a club on my arm, which for some time deprived me of the use of it, which blow had it been placed on my head, most probably would have destroyed me.

"On this a general attack was made on the men by a great number of heavy clubs and snowballs being thrown at them, by which all our lives were in imminent danger, some persons at the same time from behind calling out, 'damn your bloods—why don't you fire?' Instantly three or four of the soldiers fired, one after another, and directly after three more in the same confusion and hurry. The mob then ran away, except three unhappy men who instantly expired, in which number was Mr. Gray at whose rope-walk the prior quarrels took place; one more is since dead, three others are dangerously, and four slightly wounded. The whole of this melancholy affair was transacted in almost 20 minutes. On my asking the soldiers why they fired without orders, they said they heard the word 'fire' and supposed it came from me. This might be the case as many of the mob called out fire, fire, but I assured the men that I gave no such order; that my words were, 'Don't fire, stop your firing.' In short, it was scarcely possible for the soldiers to know who said 'fire,' or 'don't fire,' or 'stop

your firing.' On the people's assembling again to take away the dead bodies, the soldiers supposing them coming to attack them, were making ready to fire again, which I prevented by striking up their firelocks with my hand.

"Immediately after a townsman came and told me that 4 or 5000 people were assembled in the next street, and had sworn to take my life with every man's with me. On which I judged it unsafe to remain there any longer, and therefore sent the party and sentry to the main guard, where the street is narrow and short, there telling them off into street firings, divided and planted them at each end of the street to secure their rear, momentarily expecting an attack, as there was a constant cry of the inhabitants 'To arms, to arms, turn out with your guns'; and the town drums beating to arms, I ordered my drums to beat to arms, and being soon after joined by the different companies of the 29th regiment, I formed them as the guard into street firings. The 14th regiment also got under arms but remained at their barracks. I immediately sent a sergeant with a party to Colonel Dalrymple, the commanding officer, to acquaint him with every particular. Several officers going to join their regiment were knocked down by the mob, one very much wounded and his sword taken from him. The lieutenant-governor and Colonel Carr soon after met at the head of the 29th regiment and agreed that the regiment should retire to their barracks, and the people to their houses, but I kept the picket to strengthen the guard. It was with great difficulty that the lieutenant-governor prevailed on the people to be quiet and retire. At last they all went off, excepting about a hundred.

". . .That so from a settled rancour against the officers and troops in general, the suddenness of my trial after the affair while the people's minds are all greatly inflamed, I am, though perfectly innocent, under most unhappy circumstances, having nothing in reason to expect but the loss of life in a very ignominous manner, without the interposition of his Majesty's royal goodness."

ALEXANDER WEDDERBURN

Alexander Wedderburn, later Baron Loughborough, was born in Edinburgh, Scotland, February 13, 1733.

Educated at the University of Edinburgh, Wedderburn was called to the Scottish bar at nineteen years of age, and rose rapidly in his profession when he became offended by a rebuke that was administered by one of the judges.

After that, he moved to London, and was admitted to the English bar in 1757. He practiced law there until he entered Parliament in 1761.

Initially, Wedderburn supported the Bute and Grenville ministries and opposed both Rockingham and Chatham on their American policies, but found it to his advantage to briefly change his political allegiance on the issue of Wilkes in 1769.

Alexander Wedderburn
1st Earl of Rosslyn
(Lord Loughborough)
by William Owen, ca. 1798

After defending Wilkes, Wedderburn returned to the fold of Lord North. He became known as a nasty and ambitious prosecutor who put courtroom invective to the service of his own ambition. Wedderburn, who had what Lord North called "an accommodating conscience," supported North's conciliatory plans, but came to disapprove of his prosecution of the American war.

Wedderburn obtained a seat in Parliament, and on January 26, 1771, became solicitor-general in the ministry of Lord North. His position was not so much based on any sort of support for North, but rather because North decided it was better to have Wedderburn's invective on the side of the government than against it.

On January 29, 1774, when the petition of Massachusetts for the removal of Thomas Hutchinson and Andrew Oliver was laid before the privy council, Wedderburn defended those functionaries in a speech in which he made a gross attack upon Benjamin Franklin, the agent of the petitioners, stigmatizing him as a "true incendiary, and the prime conductor of agitation against the British government."

The meeting took place in a room known as the Cockpit, as cockfights had been staged there in Henry III's day.

At the same time, the news of the Boston Tea Party had reached London. Franklin was critical of this incident, as he felt that private property was to be respected. However, the news lost friends for the American cause.

Franklin later described the appearance as akin to bull baiting. However, at the time, he stood up to the tirade, displaying no emotion at all. The tactic proved successful, making him seem contemptuous and condescending of his enemies.

Wedderburn violently opposed the claims of the American colonies, and throughout the Revolution was a strong supporter of Lord North's ministry.

In 1776, Fox directed the attention of that ministry to the assumption of power on the part of the government to raise taxes in America, or annihilate charters at its pleasure, as the two principal grievances of the colonists that needed revision. In response, Wedderburn said, "Till the spirit of independence is subdued, revisions are idle; the Americans have no terms to demand from your justice, whatever they may hope from your grace and mercy."

Not surprisingly, Wedderburn was burned in effigy in Philadelphia, and regarded as one of the most unscrupulous foes to the liberties of the American people.

He became attorney-general in 1778 and chief justice of the court of common pleas in 1780. The same year, he was raised to the peerage as Lord Loughborough, Baron of Loughborough in the county of Leicester.

In April 1783, Wedderburn assisted Lord North in forming a coalition ministry, in which he was the first commissioner of the great seal. After the coalition's dissolution, he remained out of office till January 27,1793, when he became high chancellor under William Pitt.

On his resignation of that office in April 1801, Wedderburn was created Earl Rosslyn, in the county of Mid-Lothian. He became lord chancellor under Pitt in 1801. He died in Bayles, Berkshire, England, January 3, 1805. When George III heard that Wedderburn was dead, he remarked: "He has not left a greater knave behind him in my dominions."

One-hundred and forty years after Wedderburn's death, Winston Churchill "honored" the first Lord Loughborough with this now-famous quatrain:

"Mute at the bar, and in the senate loud,

Dull 'mongst the dullest, proudest of the proud,

A pert, prim prater, of the northern race,

Guilt in his heart, and famine in his face."

FOR GREATER UNDERSTANDING

Consider

1. What were the real concerns of Americans during the period leading up to the Revolutionary War?

2. Was Franklin's leaking of the letters of Hutchinson and Oliver an act consistent with his moral vision of himself and how he should act in the world?

3. What do you think was going through Franklin's mind as he silently listened to the diatribe against him by Alexander Wedderburn in the Cockpit?

Suggested Reading

Zobel, Hiller B. The Boston Massacre. New York: W.W. Norton & Co., 1996.

Other Books of Interest

Russell, Elmer B., Bernard D. Reams, and Richard H. Helmholz (eds.). Review of American Colonial Legislation by the King in Council. Buffalo, New York: William S. Hein & Company, Inc., 1981.

Websites to Visit

1. http://www.famousamericans.net/alexanderwedderburn/ - A one-page biography of Alexander Wedderburn's professional life.

2. http://www.nyx.net/~jkalb/franklin.html - A site that discusses Franklin's contributions as a "man of letters" and contains a brief description of his appearance before and after Alexander Wedderburn's diatribe.

Before beginning this lecture you may want to . . .

Read H.W. Brands' The First American, Chapter 22.

Introduction:

His dressing down before the Privy Council had convinced Franklin that his loyalties were to America and not to the British government. Now convinced that a parting of the ways was probably inevitable, he made final efforts at conciliation before at last returning to America and helping to lead the call for independence.

Consider this . . .

1. What single event most clearly opened Franklin's eyes to the fact that he was not perceived primarily as an Englishman by those in Great Britain?

2. Why did Franklin refuse to take more of a lead in writing the Declaration of Independence?

I. **Franklin remained in London for several months, hoping against evidence that the yawning gulf between the colonies and the mother country could be bridged.**

   A. The government's majority in Parliament wasn't overwhelming.

   B. Britons were as dismayed as loyal colonists at the direction of affairs.

      1. Lord Howe believed a solution could be achieved if both sides gave ground.

      2. Franklin negotiated with Howe in secret to develop a plan of compromise.

   C. But the hardliners in Parliament refused to budge, as Franklin discovered in a scornful session.

      1. Lord Sandwich called for immediate rejection of the Franklin/Howe compromise plan.

      2. He accused Franklin of being a British enemy.

   D. Franklin now had a clear impression that the British perceived Americans as being separate from the English.

II. **The colonies decided to go to war.**

   A. The British response to the Boston Tea Party—the "Intolerable Acts"—rallied the other colonies around Massachusetts.

      1. These acts were designed to punish Americans for not obeying the law.

      2. Soldiers sent to intimidate them felt to Americans like a foreign invasion.

LECTURE TEN

THE "INTOLERABLE ACTS" OF PARLIAMENT

The Intolerable Acts was a name given to a series of laws passed by the British Parliament in March 1774 as punitive measures against the colony of Massachusetts; also called Coercive Acts. Resentment of these acts contributed to the outbreak of the American Revolution a year later.

The people of Massachusetts had defied various British policies they considered repressive (they had resisted the Stamp Act in 1765) and in March 1770 had openly shown their resentment of the quartering of British troops in Boston.

After the so-called Boston Tea Party in 1773, when Bostonians destroyed tea belonging to the East India Company, Parliament enacted four measures as an example to the other rebellious colonies.

The measures were as follows:

- The Quartering Act, established March 24, 1765, required colonial authorities to furnish barracks and supplies to British troops. In 1766, it was expanded to public houses and unoccupied buildings, and was updated again June 2, 1774, to include occupied buildings.

- The Boston Port Bill, effective June 1, 1774, closed the port of Boston to all colonists until the damages from the Boston Tea Party were paid.

- The Administration of Justice Act, effective May 20, 1774, stated that British officials could not be tried in provincial courts for capital crimes. They would be extradited back to Britain and tried there. This effectively gave the British free reign to do whatever they wished, because no justice would be served while they were still in the colonies.

- The Massachusetts Government Act, effective May 20, 1774, annulled the charter of the colony, giving the British Governor complete control of the town meetings, and taking control out of the hands of the colonists.

At the same time, Parliament enacted the Québec Act, which many colonists associated with the Intolerable Acts because it expanded the territory of Québec and did not allow for representative government in that colony.

Considering these acts "intolerable," the other American colonies united in sympathy with Massachusetts. Virginia set aside a day of prayer and fasting and later proposed that the colonies meet to formulate joint action against the objectionable features of British rule. This proposal led to the First Continental Congress in September 1774.

THE

PETITION

OF THE

GRAND AMERICAN CONTINENTAL

CONGRESS,

TO THE

KING's

Most Excellent Majesty.

AMERICA:
Boston, Printed and sold at the Printing-Office, near the Mill-Bridge.

© Bettmann/CORBIS

"The Petition of the Grand American Continental Congress, to the King's Most Excellent Majesty" was presented by Franklin and other American Agents in London to sympathetic patrons in Parliament in late 1774 and early 1775. The Petition was submitted, among other reasons, as a response to the Intolerable Acts. It pledged American allegiance to the Crown, but stated that only American institutions could and should make laws for Americans. It was rejected.

B. A Continental Congress gathered in Philadelphia in the autumn of 1774 to consider options.

    1. It was modeled after Franklin's Albany Congress.

    2. It decried the Intolerable Acts.

    3. It declared the colonial assemblies the only bodies that could legislate for the Americans.

    4. It revived the boycott of British goods.

    5. But it also reaffirmed American allegiance to the Crown.

    6. The intent was to mirror the relationship between Scotland and Britain.

C. Meanwhile, the Colonial militia prepared for the worst.

    1. Irregulars mustered to defend colonists from the British, rather than from the French or Indians.

    2. When the British forces in Boston tried to disarm the Massachusetts militia (the "minutemen") a clash occurred at Lexington, and then Concord.

    3. The conflict spread all the way back to Boston during the British retreat.

D. The Continental Congress returned to Philadelphia.

    1. Delegates considered the situation in terms of this new turn of events.

    2. Turning to its only credible military leader, the Congress conferred command on George Washington.

III. **In the midst of this upheaval, Franklin returned to Philadelphia.**

A. Things had changed during his years in London.

    1. Debbie had died after an extensive illness.

    2. His son William was a distinguished British official in New Jersey.

B. Franklin was known by reputation in America, but his return was met with skepticism.

    1. Some thought he was too English after all his time in London.

    2. Never a strong public speaker, he was not impressive in debate.

C. But he proved to be as radical as anyone in the Congress.

    1. He had seen British corruption close up.

    2. Franklin's feelings showed in a letter to William Strahan, one of his oldest English friends.

        i. He outlined his anger over the way things were happening in Britain.

        ii. He called his old friend an enemy.

        iii. He wrote in a tone so angry that he finally decided not to send the letter to Strahan.

IV. **Within the Congress, Franklin stood as strongly as anyone for freedom.**

A. He proposed the Articles of Confederation, based on his 1754 Albany Plan.

B. He organized an American post office.

C. He sat on a "secret committee" to find the weapons to fight a war.

D. He traveled to Boston to consult with Washington on creating a Continental Army.

E. He traveled to Canada in an effort to persuade that colony to join the Americans.

F. He returned to Philadelphia in time to help draft the Declaration of Independence.

G. He sent a letter rejecting an offer of reconciliation from Lord Howe, now in charge of British troops in America.

H. He was dispatched to meet with Howe, who sought a personal interview.

   1. At the end of the meeting with Howe, the British commander told Franklin that if America fell he would lament it like the loss of a brother.

   2. Franklin replied, "My Lord, we will do our utmost endeavours to save your Lordship that mortification."

Summary: Franklin's return to Philadelphia marked his personal philosophical separation from Britain and was the final step toward his becoming fully American in his self-perception. Though now nearly seventy years old, Franklin threw himself into the quest for independence with the same energy he had shown in every other aspect of his life. His quiet conviction that independence was necessary helped move some people from the fence to support for colonial independence.

© Buddy Mays/CORBIS

B. Free Franklin Post Office

The B. Free Franklin Post Office was named after Benjamin Franklin and is located in Independence National Historic Park in Philadelphia.

The Articles of Confederation

Benjamin Franklin arrived back in America in May of 1775. He was elected to represent Pennsylvania in the Second Continental Congress and wrote his draft of the Articles of Confederation soon after.

See pages 501-502 of Dr. Brands' book, "The First American: The Life and Times of Benjamin Franklin" for Franklin's initial draft of the Articles of Confederation.–ed.

The Articles of Confederation was the first constitution of the United States, in force from March 1, 1781, to June 21, 1788, when the present Constitution went into effect.

They were written in 1777 during the early part of the American Revolution by a committee of the Second Continental Congress of the thirteen colonies. The head of the committee, John Dickinson, presented a report on the proposed articles to the Congress on July 12, 1776, eight days after the signing of the Declaration of Independence.

Dickinson initially proposed a strong central government with control over the western lands, equal representation for the states, and the power to levy taxes. But due to their experience with Great Britain, the thirteen states feared a powerful central government so they changed Dickinson's proposed articles drastically before they sent them to all the states for ratification in November 1777.

The Continental Congress had been careful to give the states as much independence as possible and to specify the limited functions of the federal government. Despite these precautions, several years passed before all the states ratified the articles. The delay resulted from preoccupation with the revolution and from disagreements among the states over boundary lines, conflicting decisions by state courts, differing tariff laws, and trade restrictions among states.

The articles created a loose confederation of independent states that gave limited powers to a central government. The national government would consist of a single house of Congress, where each state would have one vote. Congress had the power to set up a postal department, to estimate the costs of the government and request donations from the states, to raise armed forces, and to control the development of the western territories.

But states disagreed over control of the western territories. The states with no frontier borders wanted the government to control the sale of these territories so that all the states profited. On the other hand, the states bordering the frontier wanted to control as much land as they could.

Eventually the states agreed to give control of all western lands to the federal government, paving the way for final ratification of the articles on March 1, 1781.

The small states wanted equal representation with the large states in Congress, and the large states were afraid they would have to pay an excessive amount of money to support the federal government.

With the consent of nine of the thirteen states, Congress could also coin, borrow, or appropriate money as well as declare war and enter into treaties and alliances with foreign nations.

There was no independent executive and no veto of legislation. Judicial proceedings in each state were to be honored by all other states. The federal government had no judicial branch, and the only judicial authority Congress had was the power to arbitrate disputes among states.

> ## Article I.
> ## The Style of this confederacy shall be "The United States of America."
> ## Article II.
> ## Each state retains its sovereignty, freedom and independence, and every Power, Jurisdiction and right, which is not by this confederation expressly delegated to the United States, in Congress assembled.

Congress was denied the power to levy taxes; the new federal government was financed by donations from the states based on the value of each state's lands. Any amendment to the articles required the unanimous approval of all thirteen states.

In attempting to limit the power of the central government, the Second Continental Congress created one without sufficient power to govern effectively, which led to serious national and international problems.

The greatest weakness of the federal government under the Articles of Confederation was its inability to regulate trade and levy taxes. Sometimes the states refused to give the government the money it needed, and they engaged in tariff wars with one another, almost paralyzing interstate commerce.

The government could not pay off the debts it had incurred during the revolution, including paying soldiers who had fought in the war and citizens who had provided supplies to the cause. Congress could not pass needed measures because they lacked the nine-state majority required to become laws.

The states largely ignored Congress, which was powerless to enforce cooperation, and it was therefore unable to carry out its duties. Congress could not force the states to adhere to the terms of the Treaty of Paris of 1783 ending the American Revolution, which was humiliating to the new government, especially when some states started their own negotiations with foreign countries.

In addition, the new nation was unable to defend its borders from British and Spanish encroachment because it could not pay for an army when the states would not contribute the necessary funds.

Leaders like Alexander Hamilton of New York and James Madison of Virginia criticized the limits placed on the central government, and General George Washington is said to have complained that the federation was "little more than a shadow without substance."

On February 21, 1787, Congress called for a Constitutional Convention to be held in May to revise the Articles of Confederation. Between May and September, the convention wrote the present Constitution of the United States, which retained some of the features of the Articles of Confederation but gave considerably more power to the federal government.

It provided for an executive branch and allowed the government to tax its citizens. Congress also went from one house to two houses—the Senate and House of Representatives.

The Fight at Lexington, April 19, 1775

On April 19, 1775, British troops were met by American minutemen at Lexington, Massachusetts, where the first shots of the American Revolution were fired.

British Brigadier General Hugh Percy, who had been sent by General Thomas Gage to provide relief for the embattled British Regulars retreating back to Boston from Lexington, made this report to his superior the next day:

"In obedience to your Excellency's orders I marched yesterday morning at 9 o'clock with the 1st brigade and 2 field pieces, in order to cover the retreat of the grenadiers and light infantry in their return from their expedition to Concord. As all the houses were shut up, and there was not the appearance of a single inhabitant, I could get no intelligence concerning them till I had passed Menotomy, when I was informed that the rebels had attacked his Majesty's troops who were retiring, overpowered by numbers, greatly exhausted and fatigued, and having expended almost all their ammunition—and at about 2 o'clock I met them retiring rough the town of Lexington—I immediately ordered the 2 field pieces to fire at the rebels, and drew up the brigade on a height.

"The shot from the cannon had the desired effect, and stopped the rebels for a little time, who immediately dispersed, and endeavoured to surround us being very numerous. As it began now to grow pretty late and we had 15 miles to retire, and only 36 rounds, I ordered the grenadiers and light infantry to move off first; and covered them with my brigade sending out very strong flanking parties which were absolutely very necessary, as there was not a stone wall, or house, though before in appearance evacuated, from whence the rebels did not fire upon us. As soon as they saw us begin to retire, they pressed very much upon our rear guard, which for that reason, I relieved every now and then.

"In this manner we retired for 15 miles under incessant fire all round us, till we arrived at Charlestown, between 7 and 8 in the evening and having expended almost all our ammunition. We had the misfortune of losing a good many men in the retreat, though nothing like the number which from many circumstances I have reason to believe were killed of the rebels. His Majesty's troops during the whole of the affair behaved with their usual intrepidity and spirit nor were they a little exasperated at the cruelty and barbarity of the rebels, who scalped and cut off the ears of some of the wounded men who fell into their hands."

[The reports of scalping and mutilation were fabricated by General Percy.-ed.]

FOR GREATER UNDERSTANDING

Consider

1. How did British division on what should be done about the troubles with America help the fight for independence?

2. How were Franklin's views on character and virtue reflected in the American decision to break away from Great Britain and battle for independence?

3. In what ways did Franklin's weaknesses as a charismatic leader shape the course of the revolution? How might things have been different had Franklin been a more dynamic public leader?

Suggested Reading

Dougherty, Keith L. Collective Action Under the Articles of Confederation. Cambridge (UK): Cambridge University Press, 2001.

Skemp, Sheila L. William Franklin: Son of a Patriot, Servant of a King. Oxford: Oxford University Press, 1990.

Tourtellot, Arthur B. Lexington and Concord: The Beginning of the War of the American Revolution. New York: W.W. Norton & Co., 2000.

Other Books of Interest

Bailyn, Bernard. The Ideological Origins of the American Revolution. Cambridge, MA: Belknap Press, 1992.

Wilson, Rick K. and Calvin C. Jillson. Congressional Dynamics: Structure, Coordination, and Choice in the First American Congress, 1774-1789. Palo Alto, CA: Stanford University Press, 1994.

Websites to Visit

1. http://www.ushistory.org/declaration/related/intolerable.htm - Several pages devoted to each of the "Intolerable Acts."

2. http://www.yale.edu/lawweb/avalon/contcong/07-21-75.htm - Draft of the Articles of Confederation by Benjamin Franklin, including strike-throughs.

3. http://08016.com/wfranklin.html - Burlington, NJ, website with a short biography of William Franklin.

Recorded Books

Shaara, Jeff. Rise To Rebellion. Narrated by George Guidall. UNABRIDGED Recorded Books (15 cassettes/20.75 hours).

To order Recorded Books, call 1-800-638-1304 or go to www.recordedbooks.com. Also available for rental.

Before beginning this lecture you may want to . . .

Read H.W. Brands' The First American, Chapters 24-26.

Introduction:

Once the revolution had begun, the Continental Congress attempted to take advantage of Franklin's international reputation to drum up support for the American cause. To this end, he was sent to Paris to engage the French as allies in the American struggle for independence. Franklin quickly became a celebrity among the French leaders and people, a position that he used to secure the help the revolution would need for eventual success against the greatest military power in the world at that time.

Consider this . . .

1. What essential elements did the colonies lack at the start of the revolution if they were to have any hope of confonting the British military?

2. What decisive event helped Franklin convince the French to become involved and take the American side in what they essentially perceived as a civil war?

I. **Odds were strongly against America at the start of the revolution.**

A. It was a brave and bold thing to declare independence.

1. It meant taking on the greatest empire in the world.

2. Leaders risked a noose, or worse, drawing and quartering.

B. America had a few advantages.

1. A defensive war always favors the defender.

2. Internal lines of communication had been established.

3. Soldiers were familiar with the terrain.

C. America had greater disadvantages.

1. No navy.

2. No weapons (and a law that made weapons manufacturing illegal).

3. No industry.

4. No money.

5. Sharply divided public opinion.

i. Many remained loyal to Britain.

ii. The most bitter fighting through much of the war was between loyal colonists and patriots.

D. America's largest disadvantage was a lack of allies.

1. Franklin was dispatched to Paris to rectify this situation.

2. France was Britain's longtime enemy and seen as a likely ally.

II. **Merely getting away from America was one of the biggest challenges Franklin faced.**

A. British warships scoured the coast, especially off the ports.

　1. Their goal was to interdict commerce.

　2. They were looking to capture any official-looking parties.

B. Franklin was particularly wanted.

　1. His face was well known—better than that of any other American.

　2. He was deemed particularly a traitor, having spent so long in England.

C. He was an old man, nearly seventy-one.

Franklin In His Fur Hat

On his arrival in France in 1777, Franklin's fur hat, worn to fend off the mid-winter cold, created an instant style because of his popularity. Soon, fur hats were everywhere.

　1. He suffered from gout and other ailments of age.

　2. Younger men such as John Adams and Thomas Jefferson declined to join him on the voyage.

D. Franklin was willing to do whatever the cause required: "I have only a few years to live, and I am resolved to devote them to the work that my fellow citizens deem proper for me; or speaking as old-clothes dealers do of a remnant of goods, 'You shall have me for what you please.'"

E. To comfort him on the voyage, and in Paris, Franklin took along his grandsons, Temple and Benny.

　1. Temple's company signified the estrangement between Franklin and William, who remained loyal to Britain.

　　i. William eventually wound up in an American prison.

　　ii. Franklin refused to intercede on his behalf.

　2. Having lost his son to politics, Franklin wanted to keep an attachment to family.

F. The voyage nearly killed Franklin—it "almost demolished me."

　1. It was relatively quick, but stormy.

　2. He suffered rashes, boils, and gout.

3. He seriously doubted he could survive a return trip.

III. **Franklin's arrival in France created an immediate sensation.**

    A. He (and the boys) landed on the French coast in mid-winter.

        1. Rumors abounded regarding his purpose in coming.

            i. Some thought he was defecting.

            ii. His grandsons made it look like he was there to stay.

        2. As he moved slowly toward Paris, the speculation increased.

    B. When he arrived, he was greeted like the celebrity he was in France.

        1. His face was everywhere.

        2. Everyone wanted to meet the great man.

    C. A vogue for Franklin and America quickly developed.

        1. He arrived in a fur hat; soon fur hats were all the rage.

        2. He was on the best guest lists; hostesses fell over themselves inviting him to receptions and dinners.

IV. **Franklin proved successful in the business he had come to conduct.**

    A. Franklin appreciated the public attention, but he knew it was the King, not the public, who had the ultimate say in providing the help he sought.

        1. He needed a treaty of alliance with France.

        2. He needed money to keep the war going.

        3. With money and an alliance, the Americans stood a chance. Without them, probably not.

    B. Franklin's initial efforts helped find volunteers to serve with the American army.

        1. He was so flooded with volunteers, he soon didn't know what to do with them.

        2. Washington told him to stop sending them.

    C. Franklin's importance to the American cause was underlined by the steps the British took to spy on him.

        1. Edward Bancroft was a friend and protégé from London; he became Franklin's secretary in Paris.

        2. He reported on Franklin to the British government.

        3. He also reported on the British to Franklin, making him a double agent.

        4. Franklin took a good-natured attitude toward spying.

    D. The decisive event in shaping French support for the revolution was the battle of Saratoga, in the autumn of 1777, which showed that the Americans could stand up against the British.

        1. The news electrified Paris and paved the way to initial success in Franklin's diplomatic mission.

        2. In early 1778 he got his treaty of alliance, provoking war between Britain and France.

Summary: Though he still needed to address American concerns for money, Franklin's negotiation of the initial treaty of alliance paved the way for the ultimate success of the American Revolution within his first two years in Paris. He achieved this success largely by playing on his celebrity status with the French people and using his skill in negotiating conciliatory paths.

One of four relief panels from the pedestal of a statue of Benjamin Franklin shows Franklin at the signing of the Treaty of Paris. The statue stands at Boston's Old City Hall.

THE TREATY OF AMITY AND COMMERCE
THE TREATY OF ALLIANCE

In 1776, the Continental Congress sent diplomats Benjamin Franklin, Silas Deane, and Arthur Lee to secure a formal alliance with France. Secretly aiding the American colonies since 1775, France's helpfulness was spurred by resentment over the loss of American territory to Britain in the French and Indian War.

On February 6, 1778, France and the fledgling United States of America signed the Treaty of Amity and Commerce and the Treaty of Alliance in Paris, France.

This document was the first commercial treaty signed by the United States with any country. It promoted free trade between France and the United States.

One of the United States' earliest principles as a nation, free trade, meant that American goods would have little impediment into French markets, with the same courtesy extended to French entry into American markets.

The Treaty of Alliance was secured by the American victory over the British in the Battle of Saratoga in 1777. This convinced the French that the Americans were committed to independence and worthy partners to a formal alliance.

The Treaty of Alliance created a military alliance against Great Britain, stipulating American independence as a condition of peace, and required France and the United States to concur in any peace agreement.

Over the course of the war, France contributed money and supplies, as well as an

A Depiction of the Surrender of General Burgoyne at Saratoga on October 17, 1777

© CORBIS

THE BATTLE OF SARATOGA

The Battle, or rather, Battles of Saratoga in 1777 helped to decide the outcome of the American Revolution. They accomplished this by giving the French a reason to support the Revolution, and also permanently ended any British idea of splitting the colonies.

Early in 1777, Lord George Germain, who was responsible for British war strategy, approved a plan suggested by Major General John Burgoyne calling for Burgoyne to lead an army south from Canada to Albany, New York. A smaller expedition under Colonel Barry St. Leger would converge on Albany from the west.

By occupying Albany and controlling the Hudson River, the British intended to cut off New England from the other colonies and force an end to the American rebellion.

Burgoyne left Montréal in June with about 9,000 British and Hessian troops and a number of Native American allies. In July he took Fort Ticonderoga on Lake Champlain without a struggle and fought a skirmish with an American force near Hubbardton, Vermont.

Another British force, led by Lieutenant Colonel Barry St. Leger, marched up the Mohawk River Valley to meet Burgoyne and his men. In the battle of Oriskany, St. Leger and his men ambushed American militiamen to beat back the American forces.

On August 16, however, 2,000 inexperienced New Hampshire and Vermont militiamen defeated a detachment of troops sent by Burgoyne to seize American supplies at Bennington, Vermont.

After a three-week delay at Fort Miller (now Schuylerville, New York) to obtain provisions, Burgoyne moved his now-reduced army across the Hudson.

As Burgoyne marched his men south, the Americans destroyed bridges and chopped down trees to block Burgoyne's path and slow the British down. From the woods, Americans with rifles fired on the British soldiers. Burgoyne started to run short on food and supplies.

In August of 1777, the U.S. Congress appointed Major General Horatio Gates to lead the Northern Department of the Continental Army. Congress ordered Gates to block Burgoyne's progress, and his initial strategy was defensive, counting on Burgoyne to attack recklessly and deplete his men and supplies.

On September 13, Burgoyne began to march south toward Albany, but found his way blocked by some 7,000 Americans under Gates, who had taken up an entrenched position at Bemis Heights, a densely wooded plateau a few miles south of Saratoga.

Burgoyne moved slowly through the wilderness along the Hudson River, which gave the Americans under General Benedict Arnold time to set up a fort in a wooded area along the Hudson about forty miles north of Albany.

On September 19, 1777, British troops went over to the attack. They were met by American forces in a clearing on a nearby farm.

Nightfall and the bravery of Hessian (German mercenaries hired by King George) soldiers saved the British troops from destruction in the battle known as the First Battle of Freeman's Farm.

Ever cautious, Gates failed to reinforce Arnold and the Americans withdrew to Bemis Heights. Burgoyne made camp a mile north.

Meanwhile, St. Leger had turned back at Fort Stanwix in the Mohawk Valley. Although lacking reinforcements and commanding fewer than 5,000 men, Burgoyne refused to retreat.

On October 7 his army moved forward again in search of the American position, leading to the Battle of Bemis Heights (or the Second Battle of Saratoga). Gates's well-disciplined forces, inspired by a fearless Arnold, drove the British back to their camp with heavy losses.

Later that same day, Burgoyne attacked again. American General Benedict Arnold's leadership won the Second Battle of Freeman's Farm for the Americans. On October 17, Burgoyne finally surrendered to Gates. The Americans took about 6,000 prisoners as well as large amounts of supplies.

Aside from prisoners, the British lost about 1,200 casualties and the Americans suffered about 400. Their defeat encouraged France to join the American side and thus proved to be the turning point in the war.

Statue of Col. Seth Warner in front of the Bennington Battle Monument*

The Battle of Bennington took place on August 16, 1777, between a British raiding party and colonialist militiamen. General John Burgoyne, the Commander of the British Army, needed supplies. He sent a regiment of 800 soldiers, including British, Germans, Loyalists, and Indians, under Colonel Friedrich Baum, a German Hessian, to capture Bennington and bring back the supplies stored there.

At the same time, 1,600 New England militiamen and Vermont "Green Mountain Boys" led by General John Stark were going to Bennington to get more supplies. This group of men had been recruited by Ethan Allen and Seth Warner. When they discovered the British on the outskirts of town, they set an ambush.

Both sides called for reinforcements. Hessian Lieutenant Colonel Breymann came with 642 men and began to take control of the battle. Just when it looked like the Americans would lose, Lt. Col. Seth Warner arrived with reinforcements. After Warner's arrival, Lt. Col. Breymann lost over one-third of his men and retreated.

There were 207 British killed and 700 more taken prisoner. Col. Baum was killed in the battle. Only thirty Americans were killed and forty wounded.

The victory at the Battle of Bennington spread through the colonies, increased the morale of the continentals, and helped in obtaining aid from France.

*Note the lightning rod—a Franklin invention—atop the monument.

FOR GREATER UNDERSTANDING

Consider

1. What qualities did Franklin possess that made him indispensible for the job of negotiating an alliance with France?

2. Which is more important in deciding the outcome of wars: military strength or diplomacy?

Suggested Reading

Ketchum, Richard M. Saratoga: Turning Point of America's Revolutionary War. New York: Henry Holt & Co., 1997.

Mullin, Arthur. Spy: America's First Double Agent, Dr. Edward Bancroft. Santa Barbara, CA: Capra Press, 1987.

University Press of the Pacific (eds.). Essays of Benjamin Franklin: Moral, Social and Scientific. Honolulu: University Press of the Pacific, 2001.

Other Books of Interest

Schlereth, Thomas J. The Cosmopolitan Ideal in Enlightenment Thought, Its Form and Function in the Ideas of Franklin, Hume, and Voltaire, 1694-1790. Notre Dame, IN: University of Notre Dame Press, 1970.

Websites to Visit

1. http://www.yale.edu/lawweb/avalon/diplomacy/france/fr1788-1.htm and /fr1788-2 - Texts of both the 1778 Treaty of Amity and Commerce and the Treaty of Alliance between the United States and France.

2. http://www.patriotresource.com/battles/saratoga.html - Site with detailed information of the events leading up to the Battle of Saratoga, the leaders of both sides, and the aftermath with a bibliography. Also has links to sites with information on the principals.

3. http://www.saratoga.org/battle1777/ - A site built by persons who re-enacted the battle. It contains descriptions of the battle, images from the re-enactment, "interviews" with participants and witnesses, and links to other sites.

Before beginning this lecture you may want to . . .

Read H.W. Brands' The First American, Chapter 6.

Introduction:

Franklin's alliance with the French guaranteed that the United States wouldn't lose the war quickly, but it didn't guarantee that the new country would win. The Americans remained painfully short of cash, munitions, and ships. Franklin knew his initial diplomatic successes would be useless unless he also succeeded in the task of supplying these needs for the revolutionaries in America.

Consider this . . .

1. What techniques did Franklin use to apply indirect pressure on Louis XVI to provide support for the American revolutionaries?

2. What strategy did Franklin use in negotiating a peace treaty with Great Britain that ensured American interests were achieved?

I. **Upon completion of the Treaty of Alliance, Franklin immediately took on the task of convincing France to help supply America's other great needs.**

A. Franklin pleaded with Vergennes for the money to keep the war going and the weapons with which to fight it.

1. Vergennes was generally sympathetic to the American cause.

2. He had to deal with a monarch who distrusted revolution.

B. Negotiations with France were delicate.

1. France wanted the Americans to cause trouble for the British.

2. British anger could turn to France following a colonial loss.

3. King Louis XVI didn't want to encourage revolution within his own nation.

C. Franklin had to find a way between French hostility to Britain and Louis's suspicion of revolutionaries.

1. He appealed to the rising French bourgeois.

2. The pressure put on Louis XVI by this rising group helped gain financing for American troops.

3. He emphasized civic virtue—liberty—as the primary purpose of the revolution.

D. Franklin oversaw the activities of American privateers based in France, serving as liaison between John Paul Jones, the American naval captain, and French forces under the Marquis de Lafayette.

**John Adams
by Joseph Badger,
ca. 1770**

ADAMS AND FRANKLIN IN FRANCE

John Adams, a fellow negotiator for French aid, criticized Franklin's approach and implied that what he viewed as Franklin's "excessive civility" was not necessary on personal or political levels.

Adams suggested that the French needed America more than America needed the French. He found the French court insufferable and believed that the French would reap considerable benefits from an American victory, which they should be eager to ensure. France could expect to pick up an important new trading partner in an independent America no longer confined to trading with Britain. A defeat for Britain would also reduce its power among the premier European nations. The American victory over British forces at Saratoga, New York, in October 1777 was often cited as proof that the patriots could manage without the French. However, most of the muskets used at Saratoga by the Americans were French, as were the cannon.

French money, men, and arms helped Washington at Yorktown and secured American victory. The other American peace commissioners did not have Franklin's degree of skill, and, Franklin felt, they often bungled their tasks. The general peace concluded in January 1783 with very favorable terms for the new nation, thanks in large part to Franklin's abilities.

France, however, fared less well from the treaty. Despite Adams' insistence that an alliance with America was heavily weighted in France's favor, the expected economic and political benefits never materialized. These were major disappointments in France. A few years later, France went bankrupt. This precipitated the French Revolution.

   E. He arranged prisoner exchanges and sought to ameliorate the plight of Americans in British prisons.

II. **Whenever possible, Franklin used his personal popularity as an aid in managing the French attitude toward the revolution.**

   A. Franklin had little leverage with the French king, who wanted to keep the Americans alive but not too strong.

   B. The longer he was in Paris, the more popular he became.

      1. When Voltaire returned after decades of exile, supporters of the two men insisted that they meet. A meeting was staged at the French Academy of Sciences to the delight of the French public.

      2. A widower by this time, Franklin was especially popular with the ladies.

         i. Rumors of Franklin's conquests were much exaggerated—by himself.

         ii. But there was truth to some of the rumors.

   C. Franklin had two favorites among his French lady friends: Madame Brillon (whom he called "Brillante") and Madame Helvétius.

      1. Brillon was married, but her husband was having an affair known to all—except her.

         i. Franklin flirted shamelessly with her, writing her letters explaining why she must let him make love to her.

      ii. She enjoyed the flirtation and responded in kind.

      iii. The relationship apparently never went beyond flirtation—a game they both enjoyed.

   2. Franklin was more serious about Helvétius, a widow closer to his age.

      i. Her habits shocked John Adams and even more Abigail Adams.

      ii. Franklin pursued Helvétius.

      iii. He described to her a dream in which his Debbie and her husband were carrying on in heaven. He said upon his return to Earth: "Here I am! Let us avenge ourselves!"

III. Franklin was instrumental in finally securing the peace with Great Britain.

  A. In America, the Continental Army managed to pull itself together at Valley Forge.

   1. They gradually fought off the British.

   2. The end came at Yorktown, in 1781, when French ships guaranteed that the redcoats could not escape and Washington won a brilliant victory.

      i. British public opinion turned against the war.

      ii. While Britain could continue fighting, the war became politically unpopular back home.

  B. Franklin had the task of leading the team to negotiate the peace treaty.

   1. His fellow commissioners were John Jay and John Adams.

      i. Adams couldn't stand Franklin.

      ii. Franklin's reality did not match the image Adams had developed of him.

      iii. He was envious of Franklin's fame.

      iv. Their temperaments simply clashed.

   2. The treaty was complicated by the need to include agreements with Britain, France, and Spain.

   3. Franklin opened the bargaining with a breathtaking demand: recognition of independence, reparations, and Canada.

   4. He got independence and territory to the Mississippi, but not Canada.

   5. In 1783, Franklin signed the peace treaty with Great Britain, acknowledging, "There never was a good war or a bad peace."

Summary: In his mid-seventies, Franklin showed a shrewdness of character in the way he handled his diplomatic objectives in France. Playing to French perceptions of himself, he used his immense personal popularity with the public to apply subtle pressure that helped coerce Loius XVI into providing the colonies with the monetary and material support that enabled America to defeat Britain in the Revolutionary War.

Amorous Franklin

A letter from Franklin to Madame Brillon. He wrote this in response to Madame Brillon's flirtatious letter suggesting she could guide his soul "As long as he loves God, America, and me above all things."

Passy, March 10, 1778

I am charm'd with the goodness of my spiritual guide, and resign myself implicitly to her Conduct, as she promises to lead me to heaven in so delicious a Road when I could be content to travel thither even in the roughest of all ways with the pleasure of her Company.

How kindly partial to her Penitent in finding him, on examining his conscience, guilty of only one capital sin and to call that by the gentle name of Foible!

I lay fast hold of your promise to absolve me of all Sins past, present, & future, on the easy & pleasing Condition of loving God, America and my guide above all

Franklin playing one of his inventions—a mechanical form of musical glasses called the "armonica." He gave this to Madame Brillon, a highly accomplished harpsichord player.

things. I am in Rapture when I think of being absolv'd of the future.

People commonly speak of Ten Commandments—I have been taught that there are twelve. The first was increase & multiply & replenish the earth. The twelfth is, A new Commandment I give unto you—that you love one another—It seems to me that they are a little misplaced, And that the last should have been the first. However I never made any difficulty about that, but was always willing to obey them both whenever I had an opportunity. Pray tell me my dear Casuist, whether my keeping religiously these two commandments tho' not in the Decalogue, may not be accepted in Compensation for my breaking so often one of the ten—I mean that which forbids Coveting my neighbour's wife, and which I confess break constantly God forgive me, as often as I see or think of my lovely Confessor, and I am afraid I should never be able to repent of the Sin even if I had the full Possession of her.

And now I am Consulting you upon a Case of Conscience I will mention the Opinion of a certain Father of the church which I find myself willing to adopt though I am not sure it is orthodox. It is this, that the most effectual way to get rid of a certain Temptation is, as often as it returns, to comply with and satisfy it.

Pray instruct me how far I may venture to practice upon this Principle?

But why should I be so scrupulous when you have promised to absolve me of the future?

Adieu my charming Conductress and believe me ever with the sincerest Esteem & affection.

Your most obed't humble Serv

FOR GREATER UNDERSTANDING

Consider

1. How much did Franklin play with perceptions of his own reputation in order to achieve his political objectives in France?

2. Was Franklin's negotiating strategy with the British the most effective means of achieving the concessions he wanted in the peace treaty?

Suggested Reading

Lemay, J. A. Leo (ed.). Benjamin Franklin: Writings. New York: Library of America, 1997.

Middlekauf, Robert. Benjamin Franklin and His Enemies. Berkeley, CA: University of California Press, 1998.

Tise, Larry E. (ed.). Benjamin Franklin and Women. University Park, PA: Pennsylvania State Univeristy Press, 2000.

Other Books of Interest

Lopez, Claude-Anne. Mon Cher Papa: Franklin and the Ladies of Paris. New Haven: Yale University Press, 1990.

Price, Munro. Preserving the Monarchy: The Comte de Vergennes 1774-1787. Cambridge: Cambridge University Press, 1995.

Websites to Visit

1. http://textfiles.group.lt/etext/NONFICTION/franklin-paris-247.txt - Text of several of Franklin's letters to various correspondents, including Mme. Brillon and Mme. Helvétius.

2. http://www.dartmouth.edu/~library/Library_Bulletin/Nov1989/LB-N89-Hoefnagel.html - A web page that discusses Franklin's authorship of a poem and song—The Stol'n Kiss—he wrote to Madame Brillon.

3. http://library.thinkquest.org/22254/biopenn1.htm - A short discussion of Franklin's embassy in Paris.

4. http://www.info-france-usa.org/franceus/history/histo2.asp - The French Embassy website expresses the French view of the American Revolution and the help extended by France to the new American nation.

Before beginning this lecture you may want to . . .

Read H.W. Brands' The First American, Chapters 27-29.

Introduction:

Having achieved his greatest diplomatic success with the negotiation of the peace treaty with Great Britain that officially ended the Revolutionary War, Franklin looked to end his life of official public service. However, his great personal popularity, both in France and at home, made it impossible for him to completely leave public life.

Consider this . . .

1. What factors kept Franklin in Paris after the war that was officially ended with the peace treaty he had helped negotiate with Great Britain?

2. What vital need prompted Franklin's last official public service on the national stage?

I. **Franklin believed his job was finished at the signing of the peace treaty with Great Britain.**

A. Congress kept him on as ambassador to France.

1. The United States still needed French support, both politically and financially.

2. Franklin remained popular and respected in France.

3. Before the revolution, he had agreed to devote whatever was left of his life to the cause of American independence.

B. Meanwhile his health deteriorated.

1. Gout plagued him.

2. Even worse was a kidney stone that passed to his bladder and caused excruciating pain when he moved.

3. He could walk slowly but couldn't ride in a carriage, which jolted him.

C. He continued to work on U.S.- French relations.

Ben Franklin Holds Drawing For Bifocals

On May 23, 1785, while still in France representing American interests, Franklin wrote a paper on bifocals. Necessity was the mother of this invention—his vision had degenerated with age.

LECTURE THIRTEEN

100

1. He believed the United States owed a debt of gratitude to the French.

2. He refused to separate national morality from personal morality.

D. Even after he was released by Congress from his obligations, his French admirers, especially Helvétius, implored him to stay in Paris.

1. Not sure he could survive the journey, he was tempted to stay.

2. He wanted to return home to savor the American victory.

3. Philadelphia was his home.

4. He finally decided to go back to America to see his daughter and a grandchild he had never met.

i. Descriptions of his grandchild reminded him of Franky.

ii. He needed to feel a connection to his family once more.

E. The queen loaned him her litter, so he could be carried to the coast.

1. This assured a gentle trip.

2. It also helped get Franklin—a bad example to French people in his representation of liberty—out of the country.

Benjamin Franklin Returns from France

Benjamin Franklin is shown landing at the Market Street Wharf in Philadelphia on his return from France. He was met by cannon salutes, pealing bells, and cheering crowds.

F. He sailed across the Channel, as a test run, to England.

1. There he met, for the last time, with William, who wanted to reconcile.

2. Franklin rejected a reconciliation, citing William's refusal to follow his principal duty to his family (i.e., his father's wishes) during the revolution.

3. He asked more of William than he had given to his own family.

II. **His return home in 1785 did not provide Franklin with the retirement he had envisioned.**

A. His fellow Pennsylvanians and Americans wouldn't let him retire.

1. Partisan politics wracked Pennsylvania.

2. Both parties nominated Franklin for chief executive of Pennsylvania.

3. He was elected to three one-year terms before being allowed to retire.

B. He devoted increasing energies to his daughter and grandchildren.

C. He remodeled his house and put up two other buildings, including a print shop for grandson Benny.

Washington Presiding Over the Constitutional Convention

As delegates vie for attention, Washington presides over the discussion on the committee report that resulted in the Grand Compromise.

THE GRAND COMPROMISE

During the Constitutional Convention of 1787, large and small states were divided on the question of congressional representation.

The debate grew so heated that one Delaware delegate was heard to suggest that, for their own protection, the small states should ". . . find some foreign ally of more honor and good faith, who will take them by the hand and do them justice."

To resolve these differences regarding representation the Convention appointed a committee that recommended a compromise. This came to be known as the "Connecticut Compromise" or the "Grand Compromise."

The rationale was that the United States was, in one sense, a political society, and in another sense, a federation of separate states—parts of a unique whole.

The solution rested on the creation of a bicameral legislature. Congress would consist of two bodies: a Senate and a House of Representatives.

The compromise, supported by Benjamin Franklin, contained three important sections:

- Small states would receive equal representation in the Senate (two senators each).
- Representation in the House was based on the size of the population in each state.
- The House of Representatives was also given important powers related to taxing and spending.

To calculate state populations for House representation, each slave was counted as three-fifths of a free person (Article I, Section 2, third clause). This had been the formula used in the Articles of Confederation for the levy of federal taxes on states.

The Great Compromise also resulted in disproportional powers, favoring the smaller states in selecting the president.

Many historians believe the Great Compromise failed to resolve the longstanding rifts between the larger and smaller states and between the slave states and free (or freer) states.

If the Convention delegates had crafted a more permanent remedy for these conflicts among the states, perhaps the American Civil War itself could have been avoided eighty years later when these conflicts resurfaced.

III. **The Constitutional Convention of 1787 was Franklin's final public service on the national stage.**

A. As president of Pennsylvania, he hosted the Constitutional Convention of 1787.

B. Franklin was suggested as president of the convention, but he declined, suggesting Washington instead.

  1. He was concerned his poor health would hinder his attendance.

  2. He recognized that Washington's position as the only true national hero would give the proceedings full credibility.

C. Franklin attended nearly all sessions.

  1. He interjected rarely, always through delegates who spoke on his behalf.

  2. His intervention was always respected and became crucial to the final document.

    i. His suggestion to open sessions with a prayer was rejected, but he made his point about acting with humility.

    ii. He recommended that the president receive no salary, another failed measure that made a point about service for the good of the country.

    iii. He suggested the grand compromise of the convention, the one that produced the modern Congress, with the Senate representing the states and the House the people.

D. Though he disagreed with parts of it, Franklin strongly urged all delegates to get behind the final product and present a unanimous front to other nations.

E. His benediction on the effort lent it credibility to the public and to the world.

Summary: A full generation older than most of the other Founding Fathers, Franklin was still one of the most respected figures in America as the new nation took shape. His popularity and the respect he inspired made it virtually impossible for him to retire and remove himself from public life.

The Rising Sun

As the delegates were signing the Constitution on September 17, 1787, Franklin observed, "I have often looked at that sun behind the president without being able to tell whether it was a rising or setting sun. Now at length I have the happiness to know that it is indeed a rising, not a setting sun."

The Constitutional Convention of 1787

On February 21, 1787, Congress called for a Constitutional Convention to be held in May to revise the Articles of Confederation. Between May and September, the convention wrote the present Constitution of the United States, which retained some of the features of the Articles of Confederation but gave considerably more power to the federal government.

It provided for an executive branch and allowed the government to tax its citizens. Congress also went from one house to two houses—the Senate and House of Representatives.

Under the first constitution, the Articles of Confederation, the United States was sadly fragmented. The individual states set up customs barriers against each other, made land-grabbing treaties with the Indians, and refused to obey provisions included in the general peace treaty with England that did not suit them.

This created chaos on a continental scale until a potentially great danger known as Shays' Rebellion (named for its leader, Daniel Shays) erupted.

Small property holders in central and western Massachusetts, because of laws passed over their protests by the more prosperous legislators in Boston, were being sold out of their farms and threatened by county courts with imprisonment for debt.

In the fall of 1786, debtors prevented the courts from sitting, and in January 1787 rebels attacked an arsenal in Springfield. Since neither the state nor the central government controlled any funds with which to hire troops that would restore order, the money to do so was supplied by rich citizens.

The rebellion didn't last long, but leaders all over the nation were deeply concerned.

As George Washington wrote, "I am mortified beyond expression when I view the clouds that have spread over the brightest dawn that ever dawned upon a country."

The Continental Congress finally sanctioned a convention to meet at Philadelphia during May 1787 to officially discuss strengthening the Articles of Confederation. Actually, the idea that the meeting was intended to discretely consider the idea of developing a new government was hidden in a few minds.

Major leaders from state after state attended, including George Washington and James Madison from Virginia; James Wilson and Gouverneur Morris from New Jersey; Benjamin Franklin from Pennsylvania; Alexander Hamilton from New York; Rufus King from Massachusetts; Charles Cotesworth Pinckney and John Rutledge from South Carolina; and so on.

The plan was indeed radical. The Articles of Confederation would have to be scrapped, since they set up the Continental Congress as the only ruling body, which could, without any check, legislate whatever it pleased, administering its laws through committees made up of its own members.

The French political thinker Montesquieu postulated a theory of checks and balances. Tyranny and special privilege could be outlawed by a multiform government made up of a legislature divided into an upper and lower house, an independent executive, and an independent judiciary—all offices to be filled at different dates, for different periods of time, and according to different electoral procedures.

In order to achieve national unity, the central government would have to be enabled to collect federal taxes

The Signing of the United States Constitution

George Washington watches from his desk as a delegate signs the document. Benjamin Franklin is standing at left as other delegates observe the proceedings.

directly and to enforce federal law everywhere on the continent.

As the fifty-five convention delegates straggled in, the seven from Virginia met together to flesh out what became known as the Virginia plan. Their best orator, Edmund Randolph, presented it to the convention.

The plan committed the convention to creating a government as had never before existed, with national government consisting of legislative, executive, and judiciary branches.

Washington was unanimously elected president of the convention, and the two most important rules of procedure had been adopted.

First, every state, whether large or small, would cast an equal, single vote. The second provision was that the proceedings of the convention would be conducted and kept in complete secrecy.

This was vital, because in its most creative aspects the convention was an educational institution, where able men rubbed off rough edges, came to know and respect each other, and found paths they could travel together toward what they all agreed was an essential and invaluable goal.

As Washington put it, every delegate recognized that "something is necessary because the existing government is shaken to its foundation and liable to be overset by any blast. In a word, it is an end and unless a remedy is soon applied anarchy and confusion will inevitably be the result."

To start with, all, whether in person or through their forebears, had been set apart from their neighbors in their countries of origin by having the enterprise and courage to break away from established communities and cross a wide ocean into an unforeseeable environment.

They found themselves in a world different from any Europeans had known. Narrow overpopulated areas had given way to vastness. Very important to the Constitutional Convention was the fact that all the delegates were themselves or in immediate inheritance of self-made men, who had profited from a society where opportunity abounded, where there was no royalty or true aristocracy, where no social or economic barriers were so high that they could not be hurdled by the resolute. Furthermore, European wisdom often proved in practice inapplicable to American problems. If Americans were stumped, they tried this way and then that way until the solution was found. Improvisation was the American way of life, enthusiastically shared by the delegates to the Constitutional Convention. Their thought processes were automatically alike.

This fundamental unanimity was doubly fortunate because no decision could be effectively imposed by a majority vote, not even by a vote almost unanimous. The objective being to unify the colonies, if one state refused to accept the ultimate result, a gap that could become a festering wound would be left open.

Mutual comprehension, sympathy, and persuasion, a balancing of concession with concession, had to lead to agreement before final action was taken.

Whenever possible without weakening the total fabric, contested matters were left undetermined, to be worked out in practice when the government was in motion.

The Virginia Plan urged that legislative representation be determined by popular vote. Virginia, Pennsylvania, and Massachusetts had almost half of the population. A counting of heads would give Virginia almost fifteen times the voting power of Delaware. But the smaller states had always cast an equal vote and had no intention of being ground down. As a compromise, they suggested that representation in the lower house be by population while all states would have equal representation in the upper house.

Madison whipped up vote after vote to knock this down. Finally, a fiery delegate from New Jersey declared that the smaller states would stay out of the union, conscious that, if attacked by the larger states, they could call for help from Europe.

The convention seemed on the brink of collapse, but the delegates were unwilling to give up. A few days' adjournment was voted during which a committee would seek a compromise. This was achieved when the smaller states agreed that all financial bills would originate in the lower house, allowing the numerical majority to control the funds that fueled all branches of the government.

The most dangerous division was the dichotomy between the North and the South, a free mercantile society versus an agrarian society grounded on slavery.

Southerners feared regulation of trade might make them subservient to the North, but agreement was achieved by postponing the abolition of the slave trade until 1808. Similarly, Northerners feared that by including slaves in their population counts, Southern states would be overrepresented in Congress.

Delegates agreed on the "three-fifths compromise," which allowed Southern states to count three-fifths of their slave populations for purposes of taxation and representation.

A fundamental dilemma—how to grant adequate authority so that the executive could execute its essential role and at the same time guard against absolute rule—was defused by the existence of one man.

Washington was certain to become the president and could be trusted. It was easier to envision powers as he would apply them than to preserve alarm at what might happen further down the road. The force of the presidency that still exists is a direct heritage from Washington.

The suggestion that a Bill of Rights be included was not taken seriously. It was considered unnecessary on the grounds that, since all rights belonged naturally to the people, everything not specifically granted to the government was automatically reserved to them. A Bill of Rights was, however, added as the first ten amendments to the Constitution in December 1791.

After more than four months of deliberation, the convention ratified its handiwork by a unanimous vote of the twelve states present (Rhode Island had refused to attend). To put the results into effect nationally, it was stipulated that special ratifying conventions be held in each state and that when nine had ratified it, the Constitution would be held in force.

The strategy urged by Franklin and Washington was that no delegate would state publicly where, in achieving a necessary compromise, he had been overruled and that necessity rather than perfection be claimed.

As one state convention after another convened, the plan worked admirably.

Objections were not met by denial but by pointing out that if the difficulty proved in practice valid, the Constitution could be amended.

Over and over a majority of the delegates would be opposed when they first arrived, but the educational process that had clarified the Constitutional Convention was repeated again and again. One after another the states came in line.

This process was assisted by the publication in New York City newspapers, beginning in October 1787, of a series of eighty-five essays signed "Publius," later published in book form in March and May 1788 under the title "The Federalist," written by John Jay, James Madison, and Alexander Hamilton.

Washington, who had been at every session, thought very highly of "The Federalist."

"Upon the whole," he wrote, "I doubt whether the opposition to the Constitution will not ultimately be productive of more good than evil. It has called forth in its defense abilities which have thrown new light upon the science of government. They have given the rights of man a full and fair discussion and explained them in so clear and forcible a manner that cannot fail to make a lasting impression. Particularly the pieces under the signature of 'Publius.' "

On June 25, 1788, almost an exact month after the appearance of the second volume of Federalist essays, Washington was informed that the ninth and tenth states had almost simultaneously ratified. New York came in shortly thereafter.

Only North Carolina and Rhode Island lagged, the latter making its belated appearance in May 1790, to complete what Washington hailed as "The New Constellation of this Hemisphere."

Benjamin Franklin's Final Speech to the Constitutional Convention, September 17, 1787

"Mr. President:

I confess that there are several parts of this Constitution which I do not at present approve, but I am not sure I shall never approve them; for having lived long, I have experienced many instances of being obliged by better information, or fuller consideration, to change opinions even on important subjects, which I once thought right, but found to be otherwise. It is therefore that the older I grow, the more apt I am to doubt my own judgment, and to pay more respect to the judgment of others.

Most men indeed as well as most sects in Religion, think themselves in possession of all truth, and that wherever others differ from them it is so far error. Steele, a Protestant, in a Dedication tells the Pope, that the only difference between our Churches in their opinions of the certainty of their doctrines is, the Church of Rome is infallible and the Church of England is never in the wrong. But though many private persons think almost as highly of their own infallibility as of that of their sect, few express it so naturally as a certain French lady, who in a dispute with her sister, said "I don't know how it happens, Sister but I meet with no body but myself, that's always in the right. "Je ne trouve que moi qui aíe toujours raison."

In these sentiments, Sir, I agree to this Constitution with all its faults, if they are such; because I think a general Government necessary for us, and there is no form of Government but what may be a blessing to the people if well administered, and believe farther that this is likely to be well administered for a course of years, and can only end in Despotism, as other forms have done before it, when the people shall become so corrupted as to need despotic Government, being incapable of any other.

I doubt too whether any other Convention we can obtain, may be able to make a better Constitution. For when you assemble a number of men to have the advantage of their joint wisdom, you inevitably assemble with those men, all their prejudices, their passions, their errors of opinion, their local interests, and their selfish views. From such an assembly can a perfect production be expected? It therefore astonishes me, Sir, to find this system approaching so near to perfection as it does; and I think it will astonish our enemies, who are waiting with confidence to hear that our councils are confounded like those of the Builders of Babel; and that our States are on the point of separation, only to meet hereafter for the purpose of cutting one another's throats.

Thus I consent, Sir, to this Constitution because I expect no better, and because I am not sure, that it is not the best. The opinions I have had of its errors, I sacrifice to the public good. I have never whispered a syllable of them abroad. Within these walls they were born, and here they shall die. If every one of us in returning to our Constituents were to report the objections he has had to it, and endeavor to gain partisans in support of them, we might prevent its being generally received, and thereby lose all the salutary effects and great advantages resulting naturally in our favor among foreign Nations as well as among ourselves, from our real or apparent unanimity.

Much of the strength and efficiency of any Government in procuring and securing happiness to the people depends on opinion, on the general opinion of the goodness of the Government, as well as of the wisdom and integrity of its Governors. I hope therefore that for our own sakes as a part of the people, and for the sake of posterity, we shall act heartily and unanimously in recommending this Constitution (if approved by Congress and confirmed by the Conventions) wherever our influence may extend, and turn our future thoughts and endeavors to the means of having it well administered.

On the whole, Sir, I can not help expressing a wish that every member of the Convention who may still have objections to it, would with me, on this occasion doubt a little of his own infallibility, and to make manifest our unanimity, put his name to this instrument."

FOR GREATER UNDERSTANDING

Consider

1. Was Franklin justified in his reaction to his son William after the war?
2. How might the shape of American government have differed if Franklin had decided to spend the remainder of his life in Paris after the revolution?

Suggested Reading

Bowen, Catherine D. Miracle at Philadelphia: The Story of the Constitutional Convention May-September 1787. Illinois: Little Brown & Co., 1986.

Collier, Christopher and James Lincoln Collier. Decision in Philadelphia: The Constitutional Convention of 1787. New York: Ballantine Books (Reissue edition), 1987.

Rossiter, Charles (ed.), Hamilton, Alexander, James Madison, John Jay. The Federalist Papers. Signet Classic, 2003.

Other Books of Interest

Ketcham, Ralph. The Anti-Federalist Papers and the Constitutional Convention Debates. Mentor Books (Reissue edition), 1996.

Websites to Visit

1. http://www.yale.edu/lawweb/avalon/18th.htm - Papers related to the antecedents, debate, transmission, and approval of the U.S. Constitution.

2. http://www.constitution.org/dfc/dfc_0000.htm - Excellent site with a day-by-day calendar covering May through September of the 1787 debates on the U.S. Constitution.

Before beginning this lecture you may want to . . .

Read H.W. Brands' The First American, Chapters 30 and Epilogue.

Introduction:

Even after he left public life, Franklin spent the last few years of his life active in causes that he felt threatened the nation he had helped to establish. His legacy continued long after his death, ensuring a position in history that remains secure to this day.

Consider this . . .

1. What cause did Franklin remain active in supporting even after his official retirement from public life?

2. How had Franklin's views on God and religion changed over the years?

I. **Franklin remained active till the end of his life.**

A. Franklin finally retired after the Constitutional Convention.

1. He puttered around his house.

2. He was always happy to show off his new library to visitors.

3. He maintained his interest in science.

B. Though he left the practice of politics to others, he couldn't resist indirect involvement.

1. He continued a decades-long movement toward support of the abolition of slavery.

2. He forwarded an abolitionist petition to Congress.

3. When a Georgia congressman came to the defense of slavery, Franklin penned his final satirical piece, as from the words of "Sidi Mehemet Ibrahim," condemning attacks on the enslavement of Christians: "Let us then hear no more of this detestable proposition, the manumission of Christian slaves."

C. He also reflected on deep questions of the meaning of life.

1. Educated in the Congregationist Church, he had swung toward atheism in his younger days.

2. He gradually became dissatisfied with atheism and moved toward Deism.

i. He believed in some creative intelligence that established laws of the universe.

ii. He did not believe in an active, intervening god.

Portrait of Ethan Allen

Ethan Allen (1738-1789), frontiersman and soldier who organized and led the Green Mountain Boys during the American Revolution. (See his quote below.)

© Bettmann/CORBIS

DEISM

Deism is defined as belief in a God or supreme being, but denial of revealed religion, based on belief in the light of nature and reason. It also held that the best way to serve God was to do good to other people.

This philosophy flourished in the 17th and 18th centuries, particularly in England, holding that a certain kind of religious knowledge (sometimes called natural religion) is either inherent in each person or accessible through the exercise of reason.

The most prominent 17th-century Deists were Edward Herbert, John Toland, and Charles Blount, all of whom advocated a rationalist religion and criticized the supernatural or non-rational elements in the Jewish and Christian traditions.

In the early 18th century, Anthony Collins, Thomas Chubb, and Matthew Tindal sharpened the rationalist attack on orthodoxy by attempting to discredit the miracles and mysteries of the Bible.

Although these challenges to traditional and orthodox interpretations of Christianity aroused much opposition, the Deists did much to establish the intellectual climate of Europe in the 18th century. Their emphasis on reason and their opposition to fanaticism and intolerance greatly influenced the English philosophers John Locke and David Hume.

In France, the philosopher Voltaire became a particularly effective proponent of Deism and intensified his predecessors' rationalist critique of Scripture. Nonetheless, he retained the English Deists' view that a deity certainly exists.

Versions of Deism, some of them approaching atheism, were advocated by many other prominent figures of the European Enlightenment.

Deism was also influential in late 18th-century America, where Deistic views were held by Benjamin Franklin, Thomas Jefferson, and George Washington. The most vociferous Deists in America were Ethan Allen and Thomas Paine.

Deism in Europe and America played an important role both in exposing traditional religion to rationalist criticism and in encouraging the development of rationalist philosophy. Elements of the Deists' ideas have been absorbed into Unitarianism, Modernism, and other modern religious practices.

Excerpted from the preface to Ethan Allen's "A Compendious System Of Natural Religion"

In the circle of my acquaintance, (which has not been small) I have generally been denominated a Deist, the reality of which I never disputed, being conscious I am no Christian, except mere infant baptism make me one; and as to being a Deist, I know not, strictly speaking, whether I am one or not, for I have never read their writings; mine will therefore determine the matter; for I have not in the least disguised my sentiments, but have written freely without any conscious knowledge of prejudice for, or against any man, sectary or party whatever; but wish that good sense, truth and virtue may be promoted and flourish in the world, to the detection of delusion, superstition, and false religion; and therefore my errors in the succeeding treatise, which may be rationally pointed out, will be readily rescinded.

By the public's most obedient and humble servant.

–ETHAN ALLEN, 1784

3. When a friend inquired of his religious creed late in his life, and particularly his view of Jesus, he responded in a way that showed his evolving belief.

    i. He believed in a single, creative God.

    ii. He believed God governed the world through divine provenance.

    iii. He believed doing good was the most acceptable form of worship.

    iv. He believed the soul of man is immortal and would be judged.

    v. He believed Jesus's system of morals was the best ever devised, but that it had been corrupted by later followers.

D. His health continued to decline.

    1. His stone hurt more than ever, prompting him to take opium for the pain.

    2. The opium made his breathing shallow, which contributed to a pulmonary infection.

    3. Friends and dignitaries—Jefferson, Benjamin Rush—visited the dying man; others—Washington—wrote. "If to be venerated for benevolence, if to be admired for talents, if to be esteemed for patriotism, if to be beloved for philanthropy, can gratify the human mind, you must have the pleasing consolation to know that you have not lived in vain."

E. On April 17, 1790, at age eighty-four years and three months, Franklin died.

II. **Even in death, Franklin managed an ingenious bequest.**

A. He left an estate valued at several thousand British pounds.

    1. He established revolving funds devoted to Philadelphia and Boston.

    2. These funds were loaned out to young journeymen for five years.

    3. This would be paid back with interest.

    4. He envisioned it lasting for two centuries.

    5. Funds still existed in 1990, at which time the money was distributed for civic uses in the two cities.

B. Many years earlier, Franklin had written perhaps the most famous epitaph in American history.

C. Upon his death, he chose a simpler version: "Benjamin and Deborah Franklin 1790."

III. **Franklin's legacy continued long after his death.**

A. His individual life became the basis for the American character.

    1. He was the example of a poor boy who had made good by his own efforts, becoming a brilliant and world-esteemed success.

    2. Franklin became the archetype of the self-made man, which itself became what most Americans considered distinctive about their country.

B. His legacy includes the creation of the American republic, in which he had played such a large part.

1. His efforts to recognize his own identity led him to do all he could for his country as an Englishman.
   2. When he could no longer view himself as British, Franklin helped to create an American identity.
 C. Finally, his legacy included a recognition of the role of civic virtue in acquiring and maintaining independence.
   1. From his first days in Philadelphia, Franklin had appreciated the connection between individual development and the development of the community.
   2. He understood this during the American Revolution and during the later years of his life, when he gave himself to Congress to use him for what he was worth.

Summary: Franklin's lifetime defined a movement in America toward an individual identity. His legacy ended with a challenge to his posterity to pursue virtue with the same devotion that Franklin had shown in his own life. On leaving the Constitutional Convention, he was asked what the delegates had produced. His response clearly showed the connection between his view of individual responsibility and the new world he had helped create through his actions: "A republic, if you can keep it."

**Benjamin Franklin
by Jean-Antoine Houdon,
ca. 1780**

A Final Jab

In one of his last letters, written only twenty-six days before his death, Franklin—as "Historicus"— defends slavery to expose the absurdity of arguments in favor of the trade in human beings.

SIDI MEHEMET IBRAHIM ON THE SLAVE TRADE

TO THE EDITOR OF THE FEDERAL GAZETTE

SIR, March 23d, 1790.

Reading last night in your excellent Paper the speech of Mr. Jackson in Congress against their meddling with the Affair of Slavery, or attempting to mend the Condition of the Slaves, it put me in mind of a similar One made about 100 Years since by Sidi Mehemet Ibrahim, a member of the Divan of Algiers, which may be seen in Martin's Account of his Consulship, anno 1687. It was against granting the Petition of the Sect called "Erika," or Purists, who pray'd for the Abolition of Piracy and Slavery as being unjust. Mr. Jackson does not quote it; perhaps he has not seen it. If, therefore, some of its Reasonings are to be found in his eloquent Speech, it may only show that men's Interests and Intellects operate and are operated on with surprising similarity in all Countries and Climates, when under similar Circumstances. The African's Speech, as translated, is as follows.

> "Allah Bismillah, &c.
> God is great, and Mahomet is his Prophet.

"Have these 'Erika' considered the Consequences of granting their Petition? If we cease our Cruises against the Christians, how shall we be furnished with the Commodities their Countries produce, and which are so necessary for us? If we forbear to make Slaves of their People, who in this hot Climate are to cultivate our Lands? Who are to perform the common Labours of our City, and in our Families? Must we not then be our own Slaves? And is there not more Compassion and more Favour due to us as Mussulmen, than to these Christian Dogs? We have now above 50,000 Slaves in and near Algiers.

"This Number, if not kept up by fresh Supplies, will soon diminish, and be gradually annihilated. If we then cease taking and plundering the Infidel Ships, and making Slaves of the Seamen and Passengers, our Lands will become of no Value for want of Cultivation; the Rents of Houses in the City will sink one half; and the Revenues of Government arising from its Share of Prizes be totally destroy'd! And for what? To gratify the whims of a whimsical Sect, who would have us, not only forbear making more Slaves, but even to manumit those we have.

"But who is to indemnify their Masters for the Loss? Will the State do it? Is our Treasury sufficient? Will the 'Erika' do it? Can they do it? Or would they, to do what they think Justice to the Slaves, do a greater Injustice to the Owners? And if we set our Slaves free, what is to be done with them? Few of them will return to their Countries; they know too well the greater Hardships they must there be subject to; they will not embrace our holy Religion; they will not adopt our Manners; our People will not pollute themselves by intermarrying with them. Must we maintain them as Beggars in our Streets, or suffer our Properties to be the Prey of their Pillage? For Men long accustom'd to Slavery will not work for a Livelihood when not compell'd. And what is there so pitiable in their present Condition? Were they not Slaves in their own Countries?

"Are not Spain, Portugal, France, and the Italian states govern'd by Despots, who hold all their Subjects in Slavery, without Exception? Even England treats its Sailors as Slaves; for they are, whenever the Government pleases, seiz'd, and confin'd in Ships of War, condemn'd not only to work, but to fight, for small Wages, or a mere Subsistence, not better than our Slaves are allow'd by us. Is their Condition then made worse

Benjamin Franklin in Old Age

A 1790 profile bust engraving from Massachusetts Magazine memorializes Benjamin Franklin, "the American inventor, ambassador, and statesman." Franklin, a man famed for his versatility, wished to be remembered first as a printer.

by their falling into our Hands? No; they have only exchanged one Slavery for another, and I may say a better; for here they are brought into a Land where the Sun of Islamism gives forth its Light, and shines in full Splendor, and they have an Opportunity of making themselves acquainted with the true Doctrine, and thereby saving their immortal Souls. Those who remain at home have not that Happiness. Sending the Slaves home then would be sending them out of Light into Darkness.

"I repeat the Question, What is to be done with them? I have heard it suggested, that they may be planted in the Wilderness, where there is plenty of Land for them to subsist on, and where they may flourish as a free State; but they are, I doubt, too little dispos'd to labour without Compulsion, as well as too ignorant to establish a good government, and the wild Arabs would soon molest and destroy or again enslave them. While serving us, we take care to provide them with every thing, and they are treated with Humanity. The Labourers in their own Country are, as I am well informed, worse fed, lodged, and cloathed. The Condition of most of them is therefore already mended, and requires no further Improvement. Here their Lives are in Safety. They are not liable to be impress'd for Soldiers, and forc'd to cut one another's Christian Throats, as in the Wars of their own Countries. If some of the religious mad Bigots, who now teaze us with their silly Petitions, have in a Fit of blind Zeal freed their Slaves, it was not Generosity, it was not Humanity, that mov'd them to the Action; it was from the conscious Burthen of a Load of Sins, and Hope, from the supposed Merits of so good a Work, to be excus'd Damnation.

"How grossly are they mistaken in imagining Slavery to be disallow'd by the Alcoran! Are not the two Precepts, to quote no more, 'Masters, treat your Slaves with kindness; Slaves, serve your Masters with Cheerfulness and Fidelity,' clear Proofs to the contrary? Nor can the Plundering of Infidels be in that sacred Book forbidden, since it is well known from it, that God has given the World, and all that it contains, to his faithful Mussulmen, who are to enjoy it of Right as fast as they conquer it. Let us then hear no more of this detestable Proposition, the Manumission of Christian Slaves, the Adoption of which would, by depreciating our Lands and Houses, and thereby depriving so many good Citizens of their Properties, create universal Discontent, and provoke Insurrections, to the endangering of Government and producing general Confusion. I have therefore no doubt, but this wise Council will prefer the Comfort and Happiness of a whole Nation of true Believers to the Whim of a few 'Erika,' and dismiss their Petition."

The Result was, as Martin tells us, that the Divan came to this Resolution; "The Doctrine, that Plundering and Enslaving the Christians is unjust, is at best 'problematical'; but that it is the Interest of this State to continue the Practice, is clear; therefore let the Petition be rejected."

And it was rejected accordingly.

And since like Motives are apt to produce in the Minds of Men like Opinions and Resolutions, may we not, Mr. Brown, venture to predict, from this Account, that the Petitions to the Parliament of England for abolishing the Slave-Trade, to say nothing of other Legislatures, and the Debates upon them, will have a similar Conclusion?

I am, Sir, your constant Reader and humble Servant,

HISTORICUS.

THE "FRANKLIN" STOVE

According to the judgment of history and of their contemporaries, one of the foremost geniuses among the Founding Fathers was Benjamin Franklin.

But even geniuses make mistakes, and Franklin made a lulu with the stove he invented. It just plain did not work the way he wanted.

Franklin wanted to create a stove that gave more heat for less fuel. He designed it so that the smoke came out the bottom, which was a problem, as smoke filled the room unless the fire was kept going.

He knew fireplaces lost heat through the wall, so he designed the first freestanding stove that could be placed in the center of a room to spread warmth all around. Thick, cast iron walls absorbed heat to provide comfort even after the fire went out.

His idea was that the stove would produce more heat, but in fact the fire went out if you looked the other way for ten seconds.

Franklin did not really grasp that heat rises, and that the smoke would have to be removed through a pipe with access to the outside placed above the stove.

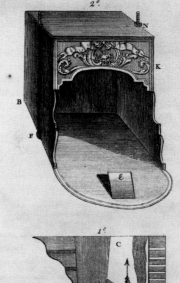

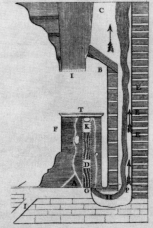

Early drawings of the Franklin stove, ca. 1760.

On the up side, Franklin noted that his family was warmer and healthier in winter time once the stove was in operation.

Eventually the stove was redesigned by David R. Rittenhouse and was in wide use by the 1790s. Quite reasonably, he called it a Rittenhouse stove. His modification was to add a long L-shaped stovepipe to create airflow through the fire and vent smoke up to a wall chimney.

By 1790, the stoves were widely used, improving the lives of early Americans. Those same stoves continue to be a fixture in American homes more than 200 years later.

But legend has its prerogatives, so the device is known as the Franklin stove.

FOR GREATER UNDERSTANDING

Consider

1. How was Franklin's work within the abolitionist movement consistent with the character values he had outlined early in his life?
2. Is Franklin's later vision of God in any way consistent with the views he held earlier in life?
3. In what ways can Franklin's legacy still be seen in America today?

Suggested Reading

Cohen, I. Bernard. Benjamin Franklin's Science. Harvard University Press (Reprint edition), 1996.

Franklin, Benjamin and Corbis-Bettmann (illustrator). Benjamin Franklin Wit and Wisdom. New York: Peter Pauper Press (miniature edition), 1998.

Walters, Kerry. Benjamin Franklin and His Gods. Champaign, IL: University of Illinois Press, 1999.

Zilversit, Arthur. First Emancipation: The Abolition of Slavery in the North. Chicago: University of Chicago Press, 1967.

Other Books of Interest

McCormick, Blaine and Neil Shifley (illustrator). Ben Franklin's 12 Rules of Management. Entrepreneur Media Inc., 2000.

Websites to Visit

1. http://www.deistnet.com/deismmen.htm - Site dedicated to the practice of Deism. Provides definitions, essays, and "Famous Mentionings of Deism," including a quote from Franklin's Autobiography.
2. http://www.findarticles.com/cf_0/m2082/4_62/64910236/print.jhtml - A short essay, citing bibliographical sources, on Franklin's religious beliefs and practices.
3. http://www.deism.org/onlyoracleofman.htm - Another Deist site. This contains the entire treatise of Ethan Allen on his beliefs as a Deist.

Editor's note: There are many hundreds of sites dedicated to or including Benjamin Franklin and the many interests and pursuits of his life. General searches list thousands. It is suggested that you narrow your searches to different categories or periods of Franklin's life to find the most useful information.

The Legacy of Benjamin Franklin

Franklin's legacy is as varied as the man himself. In the largest sense, it was presented to the nation at the end of the Constitutional Convention.

Asked by a lady in Philadelphia what the Convention's four months of secret work produced, he replied, "A republic, if you can keep it."

On a more human scale, it included his bequest of some worthless land claims in Canada, and the forgiveness of debts incurred by his son William, who stayed loyal to the British crown. His reason being "The part he acted against me in the late war, which is of public notoriety, will account for my leaving him no more of an estate he endeavored to deprive me of."

The rest of his family received various goods and flourished as their talents and fates allowed. But the trust he established to help tradespeople in Boston and Philadelphia lasted well into the 1990s, longer than the two centuries he anticipated.

Franklin remembered his own hard-scrabble beginnings, and so, "I wish to be useful even after my death, if possible, in forming and advancing other young men that may be serviceable to their country."

Accordingly, the salary of £2,000, which he had earned as President of Pennsylvania, was divided between those two cities (the lion's share to Philadelphia) in the form of a trust fund. The plan was to loan money at five percent per annum to young married men who had served their apprenticeships and were setting up their own businesses.

At the end of a century, Franklin estimated that the trust for each city would be worth about £131,000. At that time, the cities could spend £100,000 on public works, the remainder to be kept another century until it reached the amount of £4,061,000. Then the money would go into the public treasury.

In actual terms, the Boston fund was modified as the idea of apprenticeships went out of fashion. Still, at the first century mark, it was worth approximately $400,000.

Three-fourths of that money plus a matching grant from Andrew Carnegie then went to found a trade school, the Franklin Union, now known as the Benjamin Franklin Institute of Technology. The remainder of the Boston trust eventually reached $5 million, and, after some legal problems, was disbursed and the money given to the Institute of Technology.

The Philadelphia trust didn't fare quite as well, growing to only about $172,000 by the end of the first century. So, three-fourths of that bequest went to the city's Franklin Museum, which still exists as a museum of science, with the rest going to help young tradesmen in the form of home mortgages.

By 1990, the fund had about $2.3 million dollars, possibly because it concentrated on loans to poor people, as Franklin intended.

Since then, the money has been divided among the Franklin Institute, libraries, fire companies, and a group called the Philadelphia Academies that supports vocational training programs, including $300 to a 2001 battery-powered entry into the Tour de Sol race featuring experimental cars.

It was this entry, from the West Philadelphia High School, that won the "Power of Dreams Award" that year.

GRAVE OF BENJAMIN FRANKLIN

The grave of Benjamin Franklin and his family at Christ Church graveyard in Philadelphia is decorated with floral wreaths left by visitors.

The epitaph reads simply, "Benjamin and Deborah Franklin 1790." When he was young, the epitaph he thought he might use was the following:

> **"The body of**
> **B. Franklin, Printer**
> **(Like the Cover of an Old Book**
> **Its Contents torn Out**
> **And Stript of its Lettering and Gilding)**
> **Lies Here, Food for Worms.**
> **But the Work shall not be Lost;**
> **For it will (as he Believ'd) Appear once More**
> **In a New and More Elegant Edition**
> **Revised and Corrected**
> **By the Author."**

PHILADELPHIA

S Broad St

15 THE FRANKLIN INSTITUTE
222 North 20th Street
at Logan Square
(off map)

14

S 13th St

S 12th St

Locust St

Sansom St

Walnut St

**Independence National
Historical Park**
1 Independence Hall
2 Congress Hall
3 Old City Hall
4 Philosophical Hall

**14 The Library Company
of Philadelphia
1319 Locust Street**

Spruce St

*WASHINGTO
SQUARE*

S 11th St

S 10th St

S 6th St

**SEE MAP
INFORMATION DETAIL
ON PAGES 122-123**

S 8th St

Pine St

Lombard St

South St

Catharine St

Carpenter St

*Italian
Market*

0   125 m

0   400 ft

MAP OF HISTORIC PHILADELPHIA

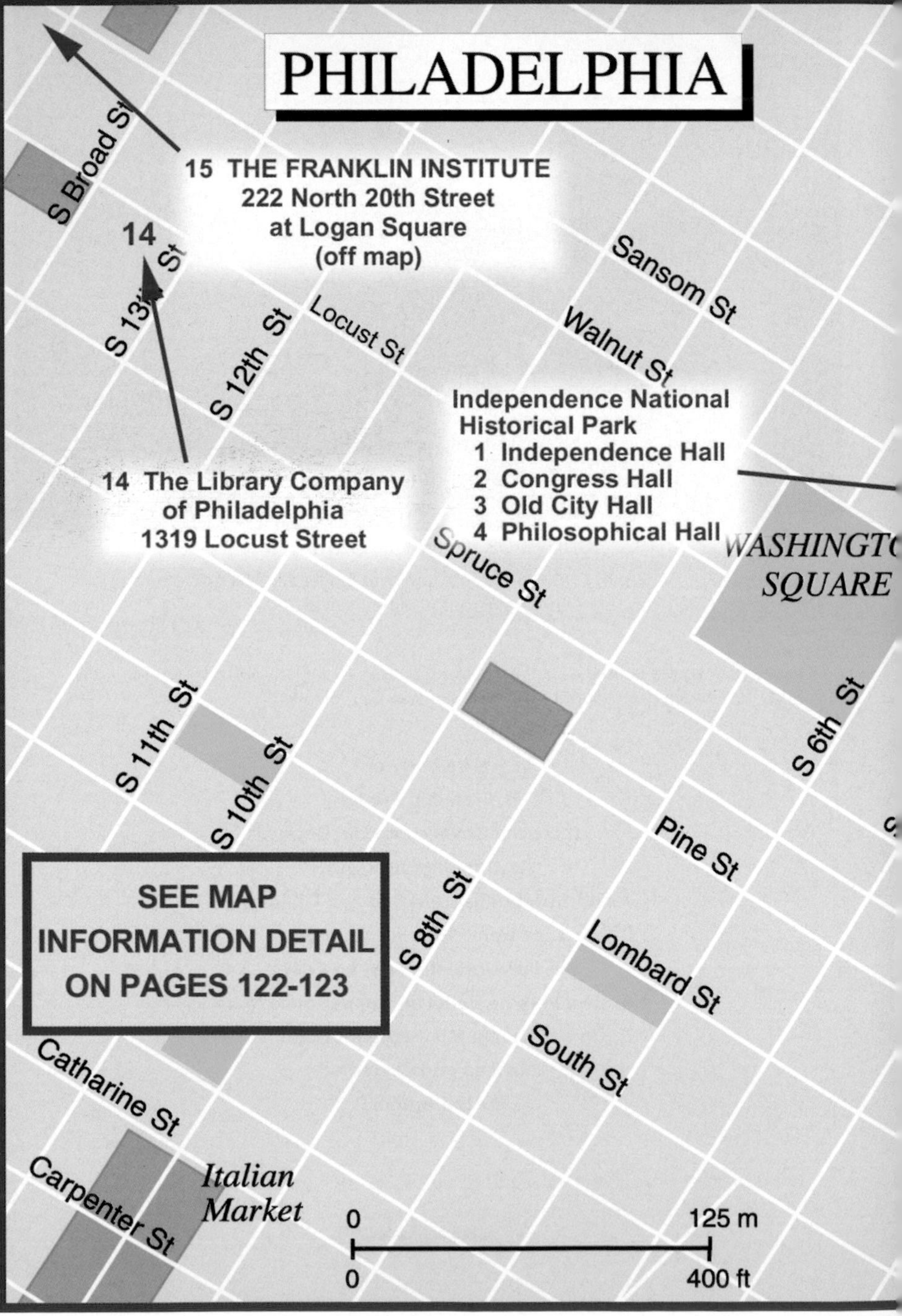

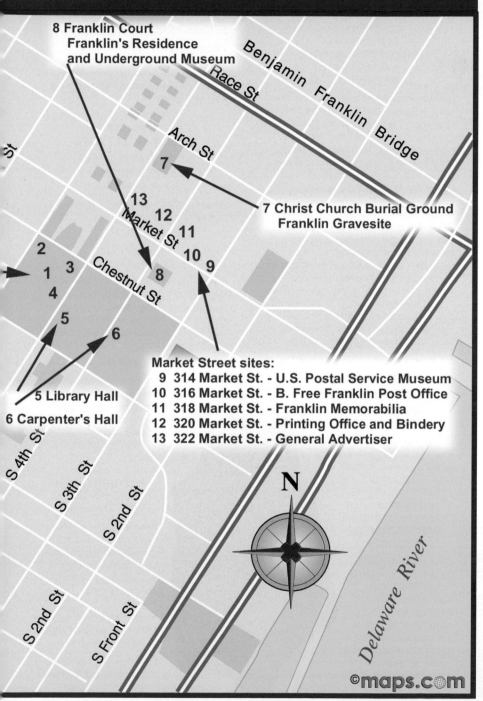

8 Franklin Court
Franklin's Residence
and Underground Museum

Benjamin Franklin Bridge

Race St

Arch St

7

13
12
11
10 9

Market St

7 Christ Church Burial Ground
Franklin Gravesite

2
1 3
4

5

6

8

Chestnut St

Market Street sites:
9 314 Market St. - U.S. Postal Service Museum
10 316 Market St. - B. Free Franklin Post Office
11 318 Market St. - Franklin Memorabilia
12 320 Market St. - Printing Office and Bindery
13 322 Market St. - General Advertiser

5 Library Hall

6 Carpenter's Hall

S 4th St

S 3th St

S 2nd St

S 2nd St

S Front St

N

Delaware River

©maps.com

Benjamin Franklin Philadelphia Map Site Information

SITES 1-6
INDEPENDENCE HALL
CONGRESS HALL
OLD CITY HALL
PHILOSOPHICAL HALL
LIBRARY HALL
CARPENTER'S HALL

Independence Hall and Congress Hall were the scenes of the First Continental Congress, the signing of the Declaration of Independence and other historical moments in American history. The Old Philadelphia City Hall is located at this site as is the Philosophical Hall (American Philosophical Society). Library Hall and Carpenter's Hall are located nearby. The Library Company of Philadelphia was located in both Library Hall and Carpenter's Hall at different periods. The Library Company was the *de facto* "Library of Congress" during the years up to and after the American Revolution until the federal government moved to Washington, D.C. Franklin laid the cornerstone for what is now Library Hall, but didn't live to see it finished. (See Site 14 for information on the Library Company's present location).

SITE 7
CHRIST CHURCH
BURIAL GROUND

Benjamin and Deborah Franklin and other members of the extended Franklin family are buried here.

SITE 8
FRANKLIN COURT and
UNDERGROUND
MUSEUM

In the Court itself once stood Franklin's house. The house was razed in 1812. Because no historical records of the look of the exterior exist, the space once occupied by the house is marked by a wonderful, oversized "Ghost Structure" designed by world-famous archi-

tect Robert Venturi and built in 1976 for the bicentennial. You can look through portals to see into Franklin's privy pits, wells, and foundation.

Below Franklin Court is a museum filled with paintings, objects, and inventions associated with Benjamin Franklin, including a reproduction of Franklin's Glass Armonica.

SITES 9-13
MARKET STREET SITES

UNITED STATES POSTAL
SERVICE MUSEUM
(314 Market St.)

Exhibits include originals of Franklin's *Pennsylvania Gazette.*

POST OFFICE
(316 Market St.)

This is the only active post office in the United States that does not fly a United States flag (because there wasn't yet one in 1775). The postmark "B. Free Franklin" is still used to cancel stamps.

318 Market St.

Here you will see an architectural exhibit about Franklin's interest in fire-resistant buildings. Walls are fully exposed to reveal wooden joists separated by masonry and plaster. In the cellar are other Franklin objects.

PRINTING OFFICE
AND BINDERY
(320 Market St.)

Demonstrations of 18th-century printing and binding equipment are on display. Printing demonstrations are given by Park Services rangers.

THE AURORA and
GENERAL ADVERTISER
(322 Market St.)

This is the restored office of *The Aurora and General Advertiser,* the newspaper published

© Richard Cummins/CORBIS

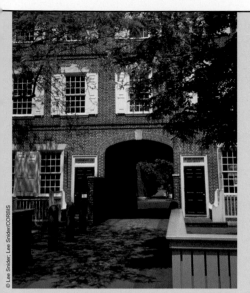

© Lee Snider, Lee Snider/CORBIS

Entrance to Franklin Court in Philadelphia

by Franklin's grandson, Benjamin Franklin Bache.

James Wilson, an editor of *The Aurora,* lived at 322 Market Street. His grandson, Woodrow, became the 28th President of the United States.

SITE 14
THE LIBRARY COMPANY OF PHILADELPHIA
(1314 Locust St.)

The Library Company's first separate structure, called Library Hall, was erected in 1789-90 at Fifth and Library Streets (just below Chestnut), directly across Fifth Street from the American Philosophical Society's Philosophical Hall. It was designed by Dr. William Thornton, better known as one of the architects of the U.S. Capitol. The building was occupied until 1878, when the Library Company moved to a much larger building on South Broad Street.

The statue of Franklin visible in the niche above the door has been restored and now sits behind glass in a lighted, street-level niche on the facade at the present location on Locust Street. The sculpture was carved in Carrara, Italy, by Francesco Lazzarini.

After Library Hall was vacated, it was razed to make room for a nondescript office building. In the 1950s, when Independence Park was created, the office building was torn down, and the Philosophical Society, then in need of a library building, put up a building on the site whose facade is an exact replica of the original building, complete with a fiberglass replica of the Franklin statue.

SITE 15
THE FRANKLIN INSTITUTE
(222 North 20th St.)

The Franklin Institute has a variety of exhibits and programs available to the general pubic. Travelers are urged to view the Institute's website (http://sln.fi.edu/visit.html) prior to their visit for travel and parking direction, up-to-date infomation on current exhibits, programs, lectures, daily demonstrations, and other details.

© Richard Cummins/CORBIS

The Benjamin Franklin National Memorial

The Benjamin Franklin National Memorial is located in the rotunda of The Franklin Institute Science Museum.

The Historic District of Philadelphia has many more interesting sites to visit such as the Liberty Bell, Free Quaker Meeting House Museum, Fireman's Hall, Betsy Ross house, African American Museum, U.S. Mint, and others.

A SHORT CHRONOLOGY OF
BENJAMIN FRANKLIN'S LIFE

1706 – Born on January 17 in Boston, Massachusetts.

1718 – Apprenticed to his brother, James, at his printing shop.

1723 – Runs away from home and ends up in Philadelphia.

1724 – Sails to London to study the latest developments in printing at the bequest of the Pennsylvania Governor.

1726 – Returns to Philadelphia.

1727 – Founds the Junto, later the American Philosophical Society.

1728 – Begins his first print shop in Philadelphia.

1729 – Purchases and begins his printing success with the *Pennsylvania Gazette*.

1730 – Weds Deborah Read Rogers.

1732 – Publishes the first edition of *Poor Richard's Almanack*.

1737 – Is designated postmaster general of Philadelphia.

1742 – Proposes the idea for the Academy of Pennsylvania, which became the University of Pennsylvania.

1748 – Retires from the printing profession.

1752 – Performs electrical studies, including the legendary kite experiment; creates the first American fire insurance company.

1756 – Is elected to the Royal Society (Britain).

1757 – Journeys to London as a delegate representing the Pennsylvania Assembly.

1762 – Returns home to Pennsylvania.

1764 – Returns to London as a colonial representative.

1772 – Inducted into the French Academy of Science.

1775 – Recalled to the colonies and named to the Second Continental Congress; presents the Articles of Confederation of United Colonies.

1776 – Plays instrumental role in drafting and signing the Declaration of Independence; undertakes secret diplomatic mission to France; becomes a member of the Pennsylvania Constitutional Convention.

1778 – Signs the Treaty of Amity and Treaty of Alliance with France.

1779 – Chosen Minister to France.

1782 – Negotiates preliminary peace treaty with Great Britain along with John Adams and John Jay.

1783 – Signs Treaty of Paris, ending the American Revolutionary War.

1785 – Arrives in the United States of America; elected President of Pennsylvania and a member of the Constitutional Convention.

1787 – Signs the Constitution of the United States of America; nominated and elected as president of the Pennsylvania Society for Promoting the Abolition of Slavery.

1790 – Dies in Philadelphia at eighty-four.

A LIST OF SOME OF BENJAMIN FRANKLIN'S
INVENTIONS AND SCIENTIFIC CONTRIBUTIONS

Throughout his life, Franklin used his keen mind in the development of creative and practical inventions and in the pursuit of scientific knowledge. He was also a pioneer in the study of electricity and world-renowned for his scientific contributions.

Inventions:

- Franklin Stove
- Lightning Rod
- Odometer

- Glass Armonica
- Catheter
- Bifocals

Ideas and Discoveries:

- **Fire Department** - In 1736, Benjamin Franklin started the first fire department: the Union Fire Company of Philadelphia.

- **Electricity** - His many experiments and inquiries resulted in worldwide recognition.

- **Fire Insurance Company** - In 1752, Franklin set up America's first fire insurance company.

- **Daylight Savings Time** - While in Paris, Franklin proposed the idea of Daylight Savings Time. By increasing the available amount of daylight during summer and decreasing it during winter, Franklin hoped to provide the world greater opportunity for doing productive work during the summer months, as opposed to the cold and dreary days of winter.

- **Gulf Stream** - Franklin was one of the first people to chart the Gulf Stream. On his several trips to Europe and back, he was able to measure different temperatures in the Atlantic Ocean and chart the Stream in detail.

- **Political Cartoon** - Benjamin Franklin is credited with creating the first political cartoon. The picture titled "Join, or Die" appeared in Franklin's *Pennsylvania Gazette*. It illustrated the Albany "Plan of Union" and his own stance on the matter.

- **Benefits of Vitamin C** - Ahead of his time again, Franklin encouraged the eating of citrus fruits such as oranges, limes, and grapefruits. He touted the advantages of fruit in maintaining healthy gums and skin. It wasn't until 1795, years after Franklin's recommendations and five years after his death, that the British navy mandated a lime in the daily diet of British seamen. The use of eating a lime proved instrumental in reducing instances of scurvy among naval crews.

You'll get the most out of this course if you have the following book:

Brands, H.W. <u>The First American: The Life and Times of Benjamin Franklin</u>. New York: Doubleday, 2000.

This book is available on-line through www.modernscholar.com or by calling Recorded Books at 1-800-638-1304.

Suggested Reading:

Anderson, Douglas. <u>Radical Enlightenments of Benjamin Franklin</u>. Baltimore, MD: Johns Hopkins University Press, 2000.

Anderson, Fred. <u>Crucible of War: The Seven Years' War and the Fate of Empire in British North America 1754-1766</u>. New York: Knopf, 2000.

Boorstin, Daniel J. <u>The Americans: The Colonial Experience, Vol. 1</u>. New York: Random House, 1972.

Bowen, Catherine D. <u>Miracle at Philadelphia: The Story of the Constitutional Convention May-September 1787</u>. Illinois: Little, Brown & Co., 1986.

Brumwell, Stephen. <u>Redcoats: The British Soldier and War in the Americas</u>. Cambridge (UK): Cambridge University Press, 2001.

Cohen, I. Bernard. <u>Benjamin Franklin's Science</u>. Harvard University Press (Reprint edition), 1996.

Cohn, Ellen R., (et al.) Editors. <u>The Papers of Benjamin Franklin—Volume I</u>. New Haven, CT: Yale University Press & American Philosophical Society, 2002.

Collier, Christopher and James Lincoln Collier. <u>Decision in Philadelphia: The Constitutional Convention of 1787</u>. New York: Ballantine Books (Reissue edition), 1987.

Dougherty, Keith L. <u>Collective Action Under the Articles of Confederation</u>. Cambridge (UK): Cambridge University Press, 2001.

Fortune, Brandon B. and Deborah J. Warner. <u>Franklin & His Friends: Portraying the Man of Science in Eighteenth-Century America</u>. Philadelphia: University of Pennsylvania Press, 1999.

Franklin, Benjamin. <u>A Dissertation On Liberty, Necessity, Pleasure, And Pain (Notable American Authors)</u>. Reprint Services Corp.

Franklin, Benjamin. <u>Autobiography of Benjamin Franklin and Other Writings</u>. New York: Penguin USA, 1989.

Franklin, Benjamin. <u>Benjamin Franklin's the Art of Virtue: His Formula for Successful Living</u>, 3rd Edition. Battle Creek, MI: Acorn Publishing, 1996.

Franklin, Benjamin and Corbis-Bettmann (illustrator). <u>Benjamin Franklin Wit and Wisdom</u>. New York: Peter Pauper Press (miniature edition), 1998.

Franklin, Benjamin. <u>Poor Richard's Almanack</u>. New York: Peter Pauper Press, 1984.

Suggested Reading (continued)

Franklin, Benjamin. The Way to Wealth. Bedford, MA: Applewood Books, 1986.

Ketchum, Richard M. Saratoga: Turning Point of America's Revolutionary War. New York: Henry Holt & Co., 1997.

Lemay, J. A. Leo (ed.). Benjamin Franklin: Writings. New York: Library of America, 1997.

Middlekauf, Robert. Benjamin Franklin and His Enemies. Berkeley, CA: University of California Press, 1998.

Morgan, Edmund S. and Helen M. Morgan. The Stamp Act Crisis. Chapel Hill: University of North Carolina Press, 1995.

Mullin, Arthur. Spy: America's First Double Agent, Dr. Edward Bancroft. Santa Barbara, CA: Capra Press, 1987.

Rossiter, Charles (ed.), Hamilton, Alexander, James Madison, John Jay. The Federalist Papers. Signet Classic, 2003.

Skemp, Sheila L. William Franklin: Son of a Patriot, Servant of a King. Oxford: Oxford University Press, 1990.

Taylor, Dale. Everyday Life in Colonial America. Cincinnati, OH: F & W Publications, Inc., 2002.

Tise, Larry E. (ed.). Benjamin Franklin and Women. University Park, PA: Pennsylvania State Univeristy Press, 2000.

Tourtellot, Arthur B. Lexington and Concord: The Beginning of the War of the American Revolution. New York: W.W. Norton & Co., 2000.

Tucker, Tom. Bolt of Fate. New York: PublicAffairs, 2003.

University Press of the Pacific (eds.). Essays of Benjamin Franklin: Moral, Social and Scientific. Honolulu: University Press of the Pacific, 2001.

Waddell, Louis M., Bruce D. Bomberger and the Pennsylvania Historical and Museum Commission. The French and Indian War in Pennsylvania 1753-1763: Fortification and Struggle During the War for Empire. Harrisburg, PA: Pennsylvania Historical and Museum Commission, 1997.

Walters, Kerry. Benjamin Franklin and His Gods. Champaign, IL: University of Illinois Press, 1999.

Zilversit, Arthur. First Emancipation: The Abolition of Slavery in the North. Chicago: University of Chicago Press, 1967.

Zobel, Hiller B. The Boston Massacre. New York: W.W. Norton & Co., 1996.

All books are available on-line through www.modernscholar.com or by calling Recorded Books at 1-800-638-1304.

Brands, H.W. The First American: The Life and Times of Benjamin Franklin. Narrated by Nelson Runber. UNABRIDGED. Recorded Books, 2000 (2 cassettes/36.75 hours).

Franklin, Benjamin. The Autobiography of Benjamin Franklin. Narrated by Adrian Cronauer. UNABRIDGED. Recorded Books, 1986 (4 cassettes/5.5 hours).

Franklin, Benjamin. Benjamin Franklin: Diplomat. Narrated by Adrian Cronauer. UNABRIDGED. Recorded Books (3 cassettes/4.75 hours).

Franklin, Benjamin. Benjamin Franklin: On Love, Marriage & Other Matters. Narrated by Adrian Cronauer. UNABRIDGED. Recorded Books (3 cassettes/3.5 hours).

Hawke, David Freeman. Franklin. Narrated by Nelson Runger. UNABRIDGED. Recorded Books (12 cassettes/16.25 hours).

Shaara, Jeff. Rise To Rebellion. Narrated by George Guidall. UNABRIDGED Recorded Books (15 cassettes/20.75 hours).

To order Recorded Books, call 1-800-638-1304 or go to www.recordedbooks.com. Also available for rental.